TT Talk

The TT's most exciting era

As seen by Manx Radio TT's
lead commentator 2004-2012

Charlie Lambert
Foreword by John McGuinness

Speedpro Series

Harley-Davidson Evolution Engines, How to Build & Power Tune (Hammill)
Motorcycle-engined Racing Car, How to Build (Pashley)
Secrets of Speed – Today's techniques for 4-stroke engine blueprinting & tuning (Swager)

RAC handbooks

How your motorcycle works – Your guide to the components & systems of modern motorcycles (Henshaw)
Caring for your scooter – How to maintain & service your 49cc to 125cc twist & go scooter (Fry)
Motorcycles – A first-time-buyer's guide (Henshaw)

Enthusiast's Restoration Manual Series

Classic Large Frame Vespa Scooters, How to Restore (Paxton)
Classic Motorcycle Restoration, The Beginner's Guide to (Burns)
Ducati Bevel Twins 1971 to 1986 (Falloon)
How to restore Honda Fours (Burns)
Yamaha FS1-E, How to Restore (Watts)

Essential Buyer's Guide Series

BMW GS (Henshaw)
BSA 350 & 500 Singles (Henshaw)
BSA 500 & 650 Twins (Henshaw)
BSA Bantam (Henshaw)
Ducati Bevel Twins (Falloon)
Ducati Desmodue Twins (Falloon)
Ducati Desmoquattro Twins - 851, 888, 916, 996, 998, ST4 1988 to 2004 (Falloon)
Harley-Davidson Big Twins (Henshaw)
Hinckley Triumph triples & fours 750, 900, 955, 1000, 1050, 1200 – 1991-2009 (Henshaw)
Honda CBR FireBlade (Henshaw)
Honda CBR600 Hurricane (Henshaw)
Honda SOHC Fours 1969-1984 (Henshaw)
Kawasaki Z1 & Z900 (Orritt)
Norton Commando (Henshaw)
Triumph 350 & 500 Twins (Henshaw)
Triumph Bonneville (Henshaw)
Triumph Thunderbird, Trophy & Tiger (Henshaw)
Vespa Scooters – Classic 2-stroke models 1960-2008 (Paxton)

Those Were The Days ... Series

Café Racer Phenomenon, The (Walker)
Drag Bike Racing in Britain – From the mid '60s to the mid '80s (Lee)

Biographies

Edward Turner – The Man Behind the Motorcycles (Clew)
Jim Redman – 6 Times World Motorcycle Champion: The Autobiography (Redman)

General

BMW Boxer Twins 1970-1995 Bible, The (Falloon)
BMW Café Racers (Cloesen)
BMW Custom Motorcycles – Choppers, Cruisers, Bobbers, Trikes & Quads (Cloesen)
Bonjour – Is this Italy? (Turner)
British 250cc Racing Motorcycles (Pereira)
British Custom Motorcycles (Cloesen)
BSA Bantam Bible, The (Henshaw)
BSA Motorcycles - the final evolution (Jones)
Classic MV Agusta Fours, The book of the (Falloon)
Ducati 750 Bible, The (Falloon)
Ducati 750 SS 'round-case' 1974, The Book of the (Falloon)
Ducati Overhead Camshaft Singles, The Book of (Falloon)
Ducati 860, 900 and Mille Bible, The (Falloon)
Ducati Monster Bible, The (Falloon)
Fine Art of the Motorcycle Engine, The (Peirce)
Funky Mopeds! (Skelton)
From Crystal Palace to Red Square (Turner)
Italian Café Racers (Cloesen)
Italian Custom Motorcycles (Cloesen)
Kawasaki Triples Bible, The (Walker)
Lambretta Bible, The (Davies)
Laverda Twins & Triples Bible 1968-1986 (Falloon)
little book of trikes, the (Quellin)
Moto Guzzi Sport & Le Mans Bible, The (Falloon)
Motorcycle Apprentice (Cakebread)
Motorcycle GP Racing in thve 1960s (Pereira)
Motorcycle Road & Racing Chassis Designs (Noakes)
Off-Road Giants! (Volume 1) – Heroes of 1960s Motorcycle Sport (Westlake)
Off-Road Giants! (Volume 2) – Heroes of 1960s Motorcycle Sport (Westlake)
Real Way Round, The (Yates)
Scooters & Microcars, The A-Z of Popular (Dan)
Scooter Lifestyle (Grainger)
SCOOTER MANIA! - Recollections of the Isle of Man International Scooter Rally (Jackson)
Singer Story: Cars, Commercial Vehicles, Bicycles & Motorcycle (Atkinson)
Triumph Bonneville Bible (59-83) (Henshaw)
Triumph Bonneville!, Save the – The inside story of the Meriden Workers' Co-op (Rosamond)
Triumph Motorcycles & the Meriden Factory (Hancox)
Triumph Production Testers' Tales (Hancox)
Triumph Speed Twin & Thunderbird Bible (Woolridge)
Triumph Tiger Cub Bible (Estall)
Triumph Trophy Bible (Woolridge)
TT Talking - The TT's most exciting era (Lambert)
Velocette Motorcycles – MSS to Thruxton – New Third Edition (Burris)

www.veloce.co.uk

For post publication news, updates and amendments relating to this book please visit www.veloce.co.uk/books/V4750

First published in April 2014 by Veloce Publishing Limited, Veloce House, Parkway Farm Business Park, Middle Farm Way, Poundbury, Dorchester, Dorset, DT1 3AR, England.
Fax 01305 250479/e-mail info@veloce.co.uk/web www.veloce.co.uk or www.velocebooks.com.

ISBN: 978-1-845847-50-0 UPC: 6-36847-04750-4

TT Talking

The TT's most exciting era

As seen by Manx Radio TT's
lead commentator 2004-2012

Charlie Lambert
Foreword by John McGuinness

VELOCE

Contents

Introduction & Acknowledgements.. 6
Foreword by John McGuinness 8

2004 – My previous visits had barely scratched the surface
Questions in parliament 10
What a way to start!.. 13

2005 – The chain's off the sprocket
Bloody-minded and unpredictable 17
Bike thieves 19
The best commentary position in the world 21
Good mates and absent friends 24
Magnificent McGuinness 27
The Manx Motor Cycle Club regrets to announce 29

2006 – Under the baseball cap was the lap record holder
Tooth and nail 33
Bad crashes and new talent 35
The slowest and the fastest.. 38
Three legs, three wheels, three wins! 41

2007 – Even the UK press gave the TT a pat on the back
Delight and despair 44
From Collier to McGuinness 46
"Switch off your brain and go for it!" 49
The land of high expectations 51
A 'mint' year 54
The first 130mph lap. 56

2008 – Manna from heaven for a live broadcaster
Too much bad news 59
Battered but not beaten 62
The flying Crowe and leathers round the ankles 65
Men from down under. 68
The Isle of Sam 70
Billown's big day 73

2009 – Rossi earned huge credit for revising his diary
Play it again, Maurice! 75
A newcomer called Jenny 78
The Rossi Posse 97
Dead or alive? 99
Electric drama .. .. .101

**2010 – The Honda coasted across the line and into Ian's own
chapter of TT history**
Old combatants 106
Hutchy's fabulous five 108
Banishing the ghosts. 113
New names in the chair 116
Sad days, strong characters . .. .117

2011 – "If anyone thinks you should call it a day, that's ridiculous"
Closer to the edge .. .. .121
Looking good, smelling great .. .. .124
"Stop whingeing" 128
Murray Walker .. .. .130

**2012 – We don't need the World Anti Doping Agency – they really
do go that fast**
The end of the Manx Grand Prix? .. .. .134
Olympic rings .. .. .137
Right people in right places. .. .. .140
Where was the fat lady? .. .. .143

2013 – A dream job for a sports broadcaster
Hitting the buffers. 146
The dream job .. .. .149

And finally, my top-twenty Mountain Course moments .. .. .151

Index .. .. .158

Introduction &
Acknowledgements

Introduction

A single lap of the TT course demands 37.75 miles of high-speed concentration. Blind corners, bright sunlight alternating with deep shadow, skimming through damp patches, bottoming out through hollows, wheelie-ing over crests – all the while knowing that split seconds can make the difference between victory and defeat.

The TT calls for courage and resilience from the competitors like no other event. They all know that the consequences of an error, or a simple piece of bad luck, can be fatal. They have all seen friends and rivals lose their lives. But still they want to race, and dream of little else all year. The TT also makes huge demands on the teams. From the logistics of transporting bikes and equipment to the island to the complex setup needed to cope with such a multi-faceted race track, the teams find the TT races the toughest of challenges.

This unique motorcycle event has been in existence since 1907. Still contested on public roads, these races weave a unique kind of magic.

The role of the lead commentator for the radio broadcasts of the TT is an exciting and fascinating one. But there's more to it. The nature of the TT, with the action inevitably taking place out of sight of most spectators most of the time, means that everyone has to tune to the radio to know what's happening. That puts the whole radio team, and especially the lead, or anchor, commentator, in a privileged position. The information must be accurate and reliable. The long broadcasts must be entertaining and reflect the different moods and emotions. And the commentators must have not just knowledge of the current riders and teams, but a deep appreciation of the history and traditions.

For nine years, between 2004 and 2012, I held the position of anchor commentator. It was a broadcasting gig like no other, starting off amid controversy and pressure, before settling into warmth and enjoyment, and then ending amid a feeling of total frustration.

This book gives my take on the events of those nine years. It is not a history of the races, which have already been comprehensively covered. Instead, it's a portrait of the TT from my perspective: the amazing characters from all sections of the paddock not just the top liners; the funny and quirky moments; the controversies which, perhaps, haven't received too much journalistic analysis over the years; and the inside story of the job as the radio commentator.

I also covered the Manx Grand Prix over the same period, plus a number of pre- and post-TT meetings at Billown, but the book concentrates mostly on the TT itself.

My time coincided with an astonishing range of records and achievements, and an equally impressive surge in recognition and popularity for the event worldwide. If I could have picked any era from the 100-plus years, this would have been it.

Acknowledgements

Thanks to the entire Manx Radio team, your comradeship and professionalism were always top class, and I hope this book brings back some great memories. Thanks especially to Andy Wint for giving me the chance in the first place; Eunice Cubbon, my producer from day one; and Tim Glover, Manx Radio's sports editor. I wouldn't have got far without you three.

Phil Wain and Chris Kinley were kind enough to put the manuscript through their expert scrutineering; particular thanks to Phil for a string of great comments and suggestions, and, I have to admit, a few corrections as well. I'm also grateful to Alan Knight for permission to use his brilliant action photos.

I'm also grateful to Rod Grainger, Kevin Quinn and Kevin Atkins at Veloce Publishing for their wise advice and for their expertise in turning my text into this impressive product.

John McGuinness is a very busy man, with countless demands on his time. I am honoured that he has written the book's foreword, and really appreciate his generous comments.

More than anyone, though, thanks are due to my wife Dorothy, for her photos behind the scenes, and for always being there: on the good days, the routine days, and the bad days.

Dedication
To Dorothy

Foreword by John McGuinness

Anyone who goes to the Isle of Man TT races year-on-year knows that a combination of factors make it not only the greatest motorsport event in the world, but also one of the greatest sporting events in general. The riders, machines, teams, and the legendary Mountain Course itself are the obvious ones, but other factors that help make the event what it is include its uniqueness, the island, and the atmosphere; and Manx Radio and the commentary team.

Over the years, the commentary became part of the TT heritage, and the voices became iconic and instantly recognisable. They carved their own impressions on the TT, and arguably became as key components as the competitors themselves. People like Peter Kneale and Geoff Cannell became legendary in their own right. Their knowledge of the TT was second to none, their enthusiasm and passion was there for all to see – and hear – and they never failed to capture the action that was unfolding in front of them. As well as all the volunteers that help keep the show on the road, they're the unsung heroes of the TT.

They played a huge part in my TT development. Nowadays we have computers and transponders and it's easy to see your sector times and where you're strong and where you're losing time. In my early TT career, all we had was the radio, and I've got loads of tape recordings of the races, and I listened to them religiously to work out where I was gaining or losing time to my rivals. By doing that, I was able to work out where I needed to improve, and there's no doubt that the information Peter, Geoff and Maurice Mawdsley gave out played a big part in my TT development.

When Peter, universally known as the 'Voice of the TT' passed away, he left a big hole in the commentary team, and some big boots to fill. The powers that be decided the man for the job was Charlie Lambert, a name not known to many bike fans, and it's fair to say the jury was out. But the biggest compliment I can pay Charlie is that he became an iconic voice at the TT in his own right. It was a seamless transition.

Straight-away, it was clear Charlie understood the TT: its heritage, its importance not only in the sporting world but also to the Manx population, and why it attracts thousands of people year after year. 'Why do you do it?' is probably the question riders get asked more than anything else, but Charlie never needed to ask that. He grasped the enormity of the event, its appeal, and what it meant to riders, spectators and the Isle of Man. Like the rest of us, he was hooked immediately. He worked hard, did his homework, made a point of speaking to all the riders in the paddock, and ensured that the picture he painted to the listening audience was as accurate and as exciting as it possibly could be.

In his time at the TT, Charlie witnessed some great racing and some landmark achievements, and I'll never forget his reaction to my 130mph lap in the 2007 Senior. I knew by the Grandstand's reaction when I came in for my pit stop that I'd broken the 130mph barrier, but when I listened to the commentary later, Charlie's reaction and words were brilliant – he almost blew off the roof!

The commentators are the eyes and ears for the teams, the wives and girlfriends, the friends and family, the fans lining the hedges, and for all those people listening around the world. Everyone wants to hear their voices, and relies on them massively to keep them fully informed; my respect for what they do is huge. For a rider flying around the 37 and ¾ mile course, commentating seems relatively easy, but believe me, it is anything but.

When I broke down in the 2008 Supersport race, rather than sulk in my motorhome, I thought I'd go up to the commentary tower to see Charlie at work. Before I knew it, he'd handed me a set of headphones, put me in a chair and told me, "Away you go." I was thinking 'how hard can this be?' but I immediately realised it was no walk in the park. The pressure of all those people listening to me was paramount and I was literally struggling for words. I was in the hot seat for only a couple of minutes, but it was a privilege to be up there and see Charlie and his team at work.

Everybody grew to like Charlie's voice, and soon realised, like Peter and Geoff before him, that he was an integral part of the TT. He understood the role he had, what part he was playing in the history of the event, and he most certainly rose to the occasion. This book gives a fascinating insight into his TT experience, so I hope you all enjoy it as much as I have.

John McGuinness

2004 – My previous visits had barely scratched the surface

Questions in parliament

It was when questions were asked about me in the Isle of Man parliament that I realised the job of presenting Manx Radio's coverage of the world-famous TT races would be different from any broadcasting challenge I had ever faced.

I reckoned myself an experienced operator in the field of sports broadcasting before I arrived on the island for my debut in May 2004. I'd commentated on everything from football's World Club Championship in Tokyo to the Open Golf Championship at Royal Birkdale. I'd reported live on TV from Canada to Malaysia, and had operated with facilities ranging from a full BBC outside broadcast unit to a mobile phone.

None of this mattered to Phil Gawne, a member of the House of Keys, the island's parliament. On the Wednesday of Practice Week he tabled a question to the Tourism and Leisure Minister, David Cretney, asking him to monitor my commentary and raise the matter with Manx Radio with a view to having my predecessor, Geoff Cannell, reinstated; and, by implication, having me fired. "Patch it up and bring him back," was the headline in the *Isle of Man Examiner*.

Geoff, a huge personality at the TT, was openly bitter at being replaced. He ensured everyone was aware of the questions asked in the House of Keys by issuing a press release about it, in his capacity as TT press officer. I had no quibble with an MHK discussing the matter if he thought it was appropriate, but I didn't think it was right for the press officer to be adding to the controversy. My role, after all, was as official announcer at the TT as well as radio presenter, and the press officer had a duty to look after my interests.

Come the Friday of Practice Week the pressure was still on. The minister had dealt with Phil Gawne's question by revealing that he had already objected to Geoff's departure, in writing, to the managing director of Manx Radio, Anthony Pugh. And he promised that his department would be monitoring Manx Radio's coverage.

It was around the same time that Des Lynam was replaced by Gary Lineker as the face of BBC TV sport. That was controversial, too, but it didn't lead to questions in parliament, or Lineker's efforts being monitored by the government. It showed how important the TT was to the Isle of Man, and how closely the activities of those involved would be scrutinised. But it was not a pleasant sensation to feel that my every cough and splutter would be analysed by politicians, and seized on by certain people with vested interests.

By the end of that first TT in the commentary box, the mood was a lot brighter. "Congratulations," said Manx Radio's programme controller, Andy Wint. "You've just completed the toughest job in sports broadcasting." From somewhere he produced a bottle of champagne: out popped the cork and we celebrated the end of my hectic, stressful debut as Radio TT's anchorman.

I looked round the commentary box as we came off air on that final day, and there were big grins on all the faces. I wasn't the only new kid on the block in 2004. Manx Radio had undergone an unprecedented upheaval at all levels, which meant that we not only had a new anchor, we also had producers, reporters and engineers who were new to the job that summer. Getting Radio TT on air and sustaining its coverage of these unique motorbike races was definitely worth celebrating, but it wasn't all down to me by any means.

My main feeling was relief, not triumph. Being parachuted into the job would have been tough enough at the best of times, but having to take over from a Manx broadcasting legend, who was still very much on the scene, was a big test.

Like thousands, probably millions, of others, I built my knowledge of the TT to the accompaniment of the name and voice of Geoff Cannell. When I began coming to the TT, as a TV reporter for the BBC, Geoff and Peter Kneale were more than the voices of the TT – they were the heartbeat of the event. You knew the races were alive and kicking the moment you heard Peter's voice, combining warmth with authority. Geoff's voice was equally distinctive: powerful, resonant, with an edge to it that seemed perfectly suited to describing the hurly-burly of motorcycle road races. One of the highlights of my career had been commentating, with Geoff, on the cycle races at the 2001 Island Games, staged on the Isle of Man. The cycling was held on the final day, just before the closing ceremony. Geoff covered one half of the course, which went in a loop from the front of the Villa Marina, up past the Gaiety Theatre, back through the Villa Gardens, and round the foot of Broadway to the Promenade; I covered the final half. The two of us combined very well, and we were even thrown into an impromptu encore when, at zero notice, we were told to commentate on the Purple Helmets' display incorporated into the closing ceremony. Up aloft on the roof of the Villa arcade, Peter Kneale introduced the whole thing with his usual aplomb.

I didn't know then that that would be last time I would see Peter. Or that within three years I would be doing his job at the helm of Radio TT. Or that within the same three years Geoff would not be involved with Radio TT at all. I would never have suspected any of it.

So, when I arrived on the island in May 2004 it was to take over the role that Geoff had performed in the two years since Peter's untimely death in early 2002. Geoff was far from happy, and wasted few opportunities to let people know.

The trouble with being a radio or TV presenter is that you are always liable to be replaced for reasons beyond your control. It had already happened to me. I used to present a sports chat show for BBC Radio 4. It was called *Seagulls Follow the Trawler*, which will give you an idea of the era. At the end of the series the powers that be decided on a shake-up, changed the name of the show and changed the presenter. I didn't feel good about it, but at times like that you just have to accept that that's showbiz.

Even so, I could hardly expect Geoff to be rolling out the red carpet for me. But I could certainly have done without the added pressure that the situation created. I'd had a hint of what might be in store a couple of months earlier when my phone rang at home. It was Geoff. "I hear you're after my job," he said brusquely. I was surprised by the call and non-committal in my response. Geoff seemed to think I should turn the job down because it would be a dirty trick to take it when he was the man in possession. But Manx Radio's decision to replace Geoff was nothing to do with me. I didn't apply for it. They offered me the job, but only after they'd decided a change was needed.

The first hint that I might become involved with Radio TT had, in fact, come in the autumn of 2001. By this time I had been working as a freelancer for less than a year, having ended 20 years on the staff of the BBC the previous February. As a freelancer, I was asked to join Manx Radio's team for the Island Games that summer. Following that, I received a call asking if I'd be interested in becoming one of the commentators out on the circuit for the TT. Fred Clarke was leaving and they were seeking a replacement. Of course I was interested. Then, in early 2002, Peter Kneale sadly died. A few weeks later the then head of the radio station, George Ferguson, rang me and offered me the job of anchor; Peter's old role. I accepted at once, only to receive a further call from George less than two months before the TT withdrawing the offer.

George, who I've known since school-days, was apologetic, but said he was being squeezed financially and had no option but to stand me down. I was disappointed but accepted the decision without complaint.

At that point I thought my involvement with the TT was over for good. The BBC in Manchester scaled down its commitment after I departed. It wasn't interested in using me as a freelance reporter, and effectively turned the clock back ten years by downgrading the TT to the sort of minimal coverage it gave it before I began championing its cause. In 2003, the TT was so far off my radar that I booked a holiday in France for the last week in May. It turned out that was the last holiday I'd be taking in May for quite some time.

What a way to start!

After two years away from the TT it was a surprise when, in 2004, I found myself packing my bags for the island once again. I knew this would be different from any other commentating job I had ever done. Football is easy by comparison. There are only 22 competitors, you can see the entire field of action, and it starts at the appointed time. The TT involves hundreds of competitors, and you see each of them for only a couple of seconds as they scorch past the Grandstand. The start could be delayed for hours. The nature of radio coverage here is totally different. So I spent weeks preparing before I even set off for Douglas: listening to commentary from the previous year, noting the areas which would present a particular challenge (when little was happening!), and researching the details of the competitors.

Geoff might have been replaced at Manx Radio but he was still very much part of the scene. He had combined the radio anchor's role with that of TT press officer. From what I understood, the radio station felt there had been too much of a clash between the demands of the two roles in 2003, which is why it had looked for a new anchor. I must say I wouldn't have fancied taking on the press officer's responsibilities as well as the commentating, and I'd wager a hefty sum that Simon Crellin, the TT press officer at the time I left, wouldn't be too keen on combining his duties with the microphone gig. In 2004, Geoff was still in post as press officer, and had been signed up as a reporter by Energy FM, the island's brash new radio station run by my pal Juan Turner. I didn't want there to be any awkwardness because it was important that Geoff and I should co-operate effectively. So I made a point to going up to the press office for the first time on my own, figuring that the guy was clearly in a difficult situation and it would be better if I didn't turn up surrounded by a gang of his former colleagues. I asked him if we could work together, and he said, "No problem." We shook hands and I thought an important bridge had been built.

It didn't really work out that way. I don't think Geoff deliberately tried to make my job harder, but there's no doubt that the situation made it pretty tricky. Confidence is everything in live broadcasting, and fortunately I have never had any problems with my confidence in front of a live mic or camera. I love the challenge and am never daunted by it. However, in between races it was impossible to avoid the undercurrents of tension that surrounded my arrival.

The Manx Radio team was called to a meeting with the race organisers. It took place in the office of clerk of the course Neil Hanson. Mike Ball of the Department of Tourism was in the chair. The objective was to impress on the radio team that we had a public service duty as well as our broadcasting responsibilities. In retrospect, this was clearly arranged so that the organisers could address themselves to me, since everyone else knew the drill perfectly well. Mike asked everyone to introduce themselves and state what their designation was. When it came to Geoff, who was there as press officer, he announced himself as "Geoff Cannell, ex-Radio TT."

Later, one of the riders, Alan 'Bud' Jackson, used a live interview with Manx Radio's Chris Kinley to call for Geoff's reinstatement. That didn't sound great in my headphones, but it was understandable. Geoff was popular with many people, and it wasn't a shock that they would want him still to be involved. I drew the line, though, when Charlie Williams, presenting our TT chat-show, read out an e-mail from a listener calling for Geoff's return, live on air. That was akin to being attacked from within. Charlie apologised and explained that he didn't know the content of the email in advance.

That was the only time the Cannell issue got under my skin, and of course that was nothing to do with Geoff personally. It came at a time when I was being asked by Manx Radio to present a number of programmes which I had not been briefed about. I was being given a lot of contradictory information about what they required me to do, all of which was eating into my preparation time for the commentaries. It was the Tuesday of Race Week and I was seriously asking myself if I needed all this hassle.

At the same time there was tangible tension between the rival radio stations. Energy's arrival gave Manx Radio a new challenge: direct competition in its own backyard. Juan had his team well briefed to provide a steady supply of interviews and updates. Having Geoff on board was something of a coup, but inevitably it also created difficulties. Manx Radio, as the host broadcaster, had paid money for exclusive rights to provide live commentary and pit lane interviews. Geoff, of course, had always been involved in that sort of full-on coverage, and my colleagues at Manx weren't amused when he continued to prowl the track-side zone during Practice Week, interviewing all and sundry for Energy. There were all sorts of complaints and threats of legal action which lasted well after the TT circus had packed up and gone home. Things were resolved eventually, but the rumpus made for a fragile atmosphere in the media centre for the entire fortnight.

Once the action started I could put all that behind me. And what action! In my very first race as Manx Radio's TT presenter the lap record for the Mountain Course was shattered.

It was thanks to the man on bike number three. John McGuinness rocketed into view from behind the trees shading the rugby field. The stopwatch told me we were about to witness history. My head told me it couldn't be possible – this was only lap one. From a standing start. The big Yamaha thundered down Glencrutchery Road. For a moment I hesitated. The last thing I wanted was to announce the wrong information. But there was no doubt. My timekeeper, Norman Quayle, was jabbing an excited finger at the clock. It read 17 minutes, 43.8 seconds. I had just commentated on the fastest lap in the 97-year history of the TT Races. What a way to start!

McGuinness' average speed of 127.68mph slashed 3.2 seconds off the previous best set by David Jefferies two years earlier. It was a phenomenal sporting achievement.

It was the start of an amazing week for McGuinness, the 32-year-old one-time brickie from Morecambe in Lancashire. The only problem he had until the Yamaha's clutch let him down in the Senior came when he arrived on the island in his motorhome. The power steering packed up as he was manoeuvring it into position in the paddock. But apart from that, he lived the dream. I'd managed to get some freelance work from BBC TV that year and interviewed him for the Beeb in the build-up. He made it quite clear that he was here to win one of the big-bike races. "I want to win either the Formula One, or the Senior," he said in his quietly-spoken, understated manner. "I feel I'm ready for it."

How right he was. Until 2004 he had won three TT titles, the Lightweight 250 in 1999, the Singles in 2000, and the Lightweight 400 in 2003. Victory in the F1, along with that lap record, took him to another level – and he cashed in by adding the Lightweight 400 and Junior 600 titles along with podium finishes in the two production races. The Isle of Man makes all-time heroes of people, and 2004 was the year that made John McGuinness the man for all seasons.

The day after his F1 win John was back on Glencrutchery Road, and I was back in the commentary box for a totally different occasion. John led hundreds of bikers round the Mountain Course in homage to the man whose record he had just taken, the late David Jefferies. DJ's death in practice at the 2003 TT illustrated how harsh the other side of the TT coin can be. The fatal accident at Crosby had occurred during Thursday afternoon practice that year. Radio TT had been due to broadcast live from Thursday practice this year, and I was determined that we should pay proper tribute to DJ, exactly 12 months on. We discussed the matter in some detail, and the plan was for me to hand over to Maurice Mawdsley, our long-serving commentator at Glen Helen, who would deliver some personal words in memory of David. Unfortunately, the rain came down, practice was washed out, and the broadcast never happened. I quickly discovered that rain and mist are the enemies of the broadcasters almost as much as the riders.

The other winners in my first year were Adrian Archibald in the Senior for the second successive year for TAS Suzuki, with local man Gary Carswell claiming an heroic podium as rain fell on the final lap, Bruce Anstey (Production 1000), Ryan Farquhar (Production 600), Chris Palmer in the last 125cc TT race held on the Mountain Course, and a sidecar double for Dave Molyneux and Dan Sayle, Dave equalling Rob Fisher's record of ten victories. All those guys continued to make headlines throughout my time in the commentary box.

That TT gave me a taste of what the event was really all about. I realised that my previous visits for TV had barely scratched the surface. This radio job, in contrast, was full-on. I'd made it through my baptism but only thanks to terrific support from Radio TT's experienced Outside Broadcast producer Eunice Crossley (later Eunice Cubbon), who kept me pointed in the right direction and ran the live sessions with cool organisation. Heike Perry also made her debut that year, presenting news and updates in German, and there was a new voice at Ramsey where former racer Andy McGladdery had the microphone. There was a good team spirit, everyone was busy, chat shows and biker-orientated music shows were coming from the Palace Hotel, other shows were out on the road, and special motorbike news bulletins were updated from the main studios. It was great to be part of it.

2005 – The chain's off the sprocket

Bloody-minded and unpredictable

Dave Molyneux provided the big success story of 2005. He also provided me with one of the most memorable moments of my commentating career – and not for the usual reasons!

Moly was the talk of the island right from the start. Even earlier than that, in fact, because he predicted that he would break the 20-minute barrier for a lap before Practice Week even began. I arrived on the island in the early hours of Sunday May 29th, after a choppy crossing on the Seacat, to find that the same winds which had caused several of my shipmates to re-examine the contents of their stomachs had also caused Saturday's opening practice session to be untimed. It was wild and woolly over Snaefell, but that didn't stop Molyneux and passenger Dan Sayle from easily breaching the 20-minute mark, even if the official watches didn't record the achievement.

It looked like TT 2005 would be a breeze for Moly in every sense of the word. But the remaining practice sessions didn't work out like that. Bad weather and problems with the bike meant that we arrived at the final pre-race practice with the sidecar favourite yet to post a single officially timed lap. The prospect of the 10-times TT champ being barred from competing was looming large. Would the organisers enforce Regulation 13, paragraph four, which stated unequivocally: "A minimum of two laps must be completed on each machine entered, one of which must be within the qualifying time?" And if they did, what would be Moly's reaction? Barely printable, if his response to the mere possibility was anything to go by.

In the end, Moly despatched all doubts in his usual straightforward fashion – by going out on Friday evening practice and blitzing the lap record; under timed conditions this time. Twice Molyneux and Sayle shattered the 20-minute barrier, their fastest time 19 minutes 31.78 seconds, 115.918mph.

The following day we turned up at the Grandstand ready for a slice of motorsport history. Instead we got a huge anti-climax as bad weather again made inroads. The Superbike TT was called off, and the sidecar 'A' race belatedly got under way at 6pm. At the end of lap one Moly and Dan had built up a 48-second lead over Nicky Crowe and Steve Norbury who were neck-and-neck in second place. But the Molyneux magic was sadly over-ridden by electrical problems at Barregarrow on lap two. Crowe and Darren Hope cashed in to take their first TT victory as we were left wondering if this was going to be Moly's year after all.

That was the prelude to the Wednesday of Race Week. Having given Molyneux the big build-up on the Saturday I decided not to tempt providence by going anywhere near the top, never mind over it, in my introduction to the day's action. When Ashley Bentley at Manx Radio's studios handed over to me at 09:45 I chose to reflect on another moment of history – the fact that it was a hundred years since the start of motorbike racing on the Isle of Man. And then, in case anyone thought I was getting a bit previous with the upcoming 2007 centenary of the TT, I quickly pointed out that I was referring to the very first event, pre-TT, which was held in 1905 to select a British team to compete in an international motorbike competition.

"In that year of 1905 they raced from Quarterbridge to Castletown to Ballacraine and back to Quarterbridge," I recounted. I pointed out that the racing back in 1905 started at half past three in the morning, and mused over the air that they must have had an even meaner producer than ours – which earned me a dig in the ribs from an indignant Eunice Crossley. "One thing that hasn't changed from day one," I continued, "is the sheer bloody-minded unpredictability of this sport." And by way of illustration, what better example than Dave Molyneux himself, after his disappointment last Saturday?

The race departed on schedule, Molyneux and Sayle leading them off in outfit number one. By the end of lap one he was, once again, in a commanding position – 33 seconds ahead of Nick Crowe and Darren Hope. And the lap record had gone – 19 minutes 44.38 seconds, 114.683mph. The second circuit was even more spectacular. Moly rocketed past us at the Grandstand, leading by over a minute and five seconds – but the statistic which leapt off the timing computer was sensational. Nineteen minutes 30.49 seconds, an average speed of an incredible 116.044mph. I remember shouting something like "Get this!" down the microphone when the time flipped up. Not exactly the style of Peter Alliss but I don't think anyone cared. Molyneux was making up for all those setbacks in magnificent style.

And so to the third and final lap. At Ramsey Hairpin (where Andy McGladdery was now sharing commentary duties with Roy Moore), he was one minute and 19 seconds ahead of Crowe and passenger Darren Hope, with Steve Norbury over a minute further back. The pick-up points across the mountain flashed back the read-outs as the transponder on outfit number one scorched past. Past the Bungalow, through our monitor providing pictures from Creg ny Baa, and past Cronk ny Mona where the computer registered his passage just as the green light flicked on above No 1 on the scoreboard opposite. I was winding myself up to give him a suitable greeting as he crossed the line. I'd given some thought beforehand to a suitable line, and planned to say something about Sir Steve Redgrave, Ian Botham and Martin O'Neill being left in Molyneux's slipstream when it came to sporting legends. It seemed to be taking an awful long time for the hero of the hour to reach us from Cronk ny Mona. I looked for the telltale sign of Andy Fern preparing the chequered flag. And suddenly there was Molyneux – but something was wrong! Far from flashing down the centre of the road he was coasting towards the finish. He'd pulled over towards the right-hand side of the track as we looked up Glencrutchery Road. My carefully-rehearsed salutation was forgotten, and I was left to exclaim a somewhat unpoetic "Oh my goodness!" Well, what else do you say in a situation like that? I imagine Moly was saying something even less poetic. All I could do was describe what I was seeing, which was outfit number one passing slowly in front of us with both driver and passenger peering down towards the base of the machine, clearly worried about some mechanical problem. A dozen thoughts sprinted through my mind, among them: how much time had they lost? Could Crowe and Hope catch them now? Fortunately, I instantly realised that that was out of the question, and was able to welcome them as winners. Even with the slow-down Moly had smashed the 20-minute mark for the third time, and breached the hour mark for the race – a new record of 59 minutes 06.39 seconds. But what a moment. And what a finish! The old boys who set out at half past three in the morning a hundred years earlier would have understood. The sport may be faster these days, but in many ways it hasn't changed at all.

Bike thieves

2005 was nothing like as tricky as the year before. I'd been through the mill and found out how the system worked. I knew the other people involved. I felt as if I could shed the metaphorical orange jacket of the newcomer and relax – slightly. You can never afford to be too relaxed in live broadcasting. Much like riding a motorbike, you have to be alert all the time. You also have to be fully prepared, and that means finding out as much as you can about the personalities.

Within a day of arriving on the island I was invited by Brian Rostron to an evening gathering at his lovely home overlooking Laxey Bay. I'd filmed Brian in the past for a *North West Tonight* report – as a Merseysider who was still competing in sidecars beyond his 60th birthday, Brian made a great subject for a human interest report. This year Brian was stomping around like a caged leopard, struggling to come to terms with the fact that a major operation prevented him from racing. But he was still very much involved. He might have been out of commission but his outfit was in the thick of it. Among the other guests at the do organised by Brian and his wife Ann was another veteran campaigner, Dick Hawes. Dick was driving Brian's bike this year, and the story of how the arrangement came about was one of those which is both typical of the TT and also typical of the sort of reporting I thought I could bring to the radio coverage.

Dick recounted to me how he spent a lot of time racing on the Continent, especially Belgium. One evening a few weeks previously he had parked up at a motorway service station on the M25 to catch forty winks. He awoke to find thieves had struck while he was asleep. They'd uncoupled the trailer containing his sidecar outfit and made off with it – and three spare engines as well. The mind boggles at the thought of a couple of desperate villains using Dick Hawes' racing sidecar as their next getaway vehicle. The police hadn't traced it, so Dick was preparing to withdraw his entry. All somewhat ironic bearing in mind that Dick, originally from Dartford but then living in Ramsey, was the boss of a security company!

At that point Brian stepped in and offered him his own machine, which meant one of the TT's long-serving troubadours could carry on and compete in his 39th TT. Dick took tenth place in the 1969 Sidecar World Championship on a Seeley, the last time a British machine finished in the top ten at that level. He took third place at the TT in 1974 on a works Weslake when the event counted towards the world standings, and, in 1993, he was third overall at the TT. He has ridden solos and passengered at the TT, and now here he was, despite all the problems, lining up again, with Eddie Kiff in the chair. Dick was to go on to finish both races, bringing the Rostron machine home in 31st and 29th places.

Fiona Baker-Milligan was another of Brian and Ann's guests that evening. Fiona was one of the most recognisable characters in the paddock – tall, lithe as befitted a trampoline instructor, with a shock of blonde hair. I'd met Fiona the previous year when she was making her TT debut as passenger to Mick Harvey. These two demonstrated another of the familiar aspects of the TT, the family connections woven through the entire event like threads in a tapestry. Mick, approaching his 60th birthday when he raced in 2005, is the father of solo competitor Phil

Harvey while Fiona is the daughter of sidecar driver and designer Tony Baker. For the second year running Fiona and Mick were drawn to start directly in front of Tony. Fiona told me how she'd stuck a sign on the rear of their outfit reading 'No Overtaking,' for the benefit of dad Tony. Once she'd got the idea there was no stopping her. Does my bum look big in this? was another of the signs she came up with.

It's a good job she could see the bright side because her first year at the TT came to an alarming end when the machine caught fire at the end of the Cronk y Voddy straight in Race B. "Flames shot up my arms, and there was smoke everywhere," she recalled. But it would take a lot worse than that to deter this action-woman. As well as teaching trampoline skills, Fiona is a former captain of Kendal Athletics Club in the Lake District. She began sidecar racing in 2003 when Mick lost his regular passenger Steve Taylor to injury. At the end of that season she was awarded the Aaron Kennedy Trophy for the best new passenger in the Formula 2 National Championship. 2004 in the Isle of Man saw the duo take 16th place in Race A before their challenge in Race B ended on Cronk y Voddy. In 2005, Fiona went a couple of places better, taking 14th place in Race B after finishing 26th in Race A. Mick, of course, is a highly experienced TT driver, having a best finish of sixth in 2000. But it was Fiona's dad who had the last laugh. Ignoring his daughter's warning signs, Tony got past Mick and Fiona in each race and took creditable sixth and eighth places, earning silver and bronze replicas, respectively, and almost matching his best-ever finish of fifth from 2003. It was good to be able to chat to people like Brian, Dick and Fiona in relaxed circumstances.

The best commentary position in the world

Manx Radio seemed a smoother operation all round in 2005. It must have helped that it had had a year's experience after the big shake-up of 2004. There were no unexpected surprises for me, no shows to present at a moment's notice, and no pressure to divert me from my preparations. In fact, before the end of Practice Week, I was in danger of becoming what the racehorse fraternity might call 'over-trained' – all preparation and no serious action! I readily put my hand up for some unscheduled commentating, although it wouldn't come into effect until after the TT. Maurice Mawdsley was unavailable for the post-TT Steam Packet races at Billown, so I volunteered. I'd watched Maurice in action at the pre-TT Classic for two years so I thought it would be pretty easy. Of course, it wasn't. Come the day, I discovered that the organisers didn't wait for the appointed hour to start each race – as soon as the riders were on the grid, off they went. So the start of the first race caught me on the hop. I'd grabbed a good eyeful of the computer system at the Classic races – it's a fantastic system which gives the commentator the exact splits between each rider as they pass the start/finish line. That part of the job went fine, but inevitably there were other details which I hadn't noticed, and it was somewhat embarrassing when I failed to pick up on the fact that Ian Lougher had retired on the last lap of one race. It was complicated by the race being run as two concurrent classes. I'd called home the first three in one class but was still waiting for Lougher to take the second win, oblivious to the appearance of two other riders passing by to claim the top two places.

Apart from those hiccups I thoroughly enjoyed the stint at Billown. The officials of the Southern 100 Club look after the media exceptionally well, especially Trisha Clague who kept me plied with so many cakes, sandwiches and chocolate biscuits it was a wonder I was able to find time to commentate at all! Not that that explained my forgetting to flick the little red switch to activate the microphone early-on in the proceedings. Bob Allison, the Manx Radio engineer, had given me a briefing beforehand. The radio kit was similar to the kit I used for football reports for the BBC but with the significant addition of this red switch which I had to flick to activate the mic. When my fellow commentator Roy Moore, stationed out at Cross Four Ways, handed back to me early in the first race I launched into a high-octane description of Ryan Farquhar scorching past me on the Kawasaki, blissfully ignorant of the fact that no-one else was hearing the commentary. The brain must have well and truly parked because I heard Chris Williams in the studio, via my headphones, shouting to Chris Kinley to take over the commentary and I still didn't twig. Chris must have had his cans off because he didn't respond. Suddenly there was a blur of motion in the commentary box as Bob rushed in and threw the red switch. I was back on the air, face almost as red as the wretched switch! All I could do was apologise to the listeners and confess that the mistake was entirely my responsibility. I also took the opportunity to tell them that they'd missed some of the best motorsport commentary ever, secure in the knowledge that no-one would ever be able to dispute the claim!

It didn't help that the commentary box at Billown is squarely in the public view. At most sporting events the commentators are out of the way on gantries or at the very rear of the stands. Here, the position is directly opposite the small grandstand which, on this day, was packed. My mistake was horribly public.

Despite that, I quickly christened Billown as the best commentary position in the world. The reason is because it's so close to the track. The view from the TT Grandstand is panoramic, but we are so high up the tower that you feel remote from the action. At the Southern 100 course you are so close you could, as I mentioned in my commentary that day, lean out of the window to check if the riders had brushed their teeth that morning. The view as they hurtle towards the finishing line is as good as that enjoyed by the official with the chequered flag. You even get a handy warning that the riders are about to come into view because you can spot them on the distant railway bridge just before they take the final right-hander at Castletown Corner to complete the lap. I've worked in commentary boxes throughout the Premier League and in many countries, from the Parc des Princes in Paris to the Olympic Stadium in Tokyo, and there isn't one which gives you quite the buzz as the start/finish line at Billown in the Isle of Man. So long as you remember to turn on that little red switch.

Unfortunately, the episode at Billown wasn't the last of my embarrassing episodes that year. Foreshortening the career of the Lieutenant Governor of the Isle of Man is usually the sole prerogative of the Queen. So it was unfortunate, to say the least, that I inadvertently took over Her Majesty's duties.

One of the rituals of the TT is that the Governor is driven from his mansion along Glencrutchery Road, arriving some 30 minutes or so before the start of racing. His appearance is always marked by a formal welcome from the race officials and the playing of the National Anthem – and it's also tradition that Radio TT provides live commentary of the event.

Having kept an eye on news stories from the island since my previous visit I was aware that a successor had been announced to the man in post last year, Air Marshal Ian Macfadyen. Preparing for the day's commentary up in the box I asked if the new Governor was in post yet and whether anyone knew his name. No-one knew the name. Someone beetled off to the media centre below to find out and duly returned with the name Peter Haddacks scrawled on a piece of paper. Accordingly, as the limousine progressed towards its dropping-off point, I proclaimed the arrival of the new Lieutenant Governor Peter Haddacks on the occasion of his first TT. The door opened and out stepped ... the familiar figure of Air Marshal Ian Macfadyen CB OBE. Oh dear, oh dear! How do I wriggle out of that one? Not that I was blaming my messenger. He'd been asked to find out the name of the new Governor and that is what he had done. But somewhere there'd been an absence of putting two and two together. I had to apologise for the misunderstanding and quickly set the record straight but it was a pretty bad moment. Another one came about half an hour later when the Air Marshal himself showed up in the commentary box! I thought I was in for at least a dozen lashes but he greeted us all cheerily, didn't say a word about my gaffe, beamed at one and all, and moved on to visit the police box.

It's always been one of my mantras in broadcasting that you

shouldn't worry about making mistakes, because mistakes are inevitable when you're live on air – it's how you deal with the mistakes that counts. That, however, was a bad mistake and there was no clear way to deal with it except to carry on with as much confidence as possible. It turned out that Ian Macfadyen was still around at the Manx later that year – although that was, definitely, his farewell appearance on the Mountain Course.

Good mates and absent friends

I shouldn't give the impression that presenting Radio TT's coverage is like some sort of monastic existence, studying and concentrating. There's plenty of time for fun. That's what the TT is for, isn't it? The great thing about it is that no-one has to get intoxicated to enjoy themselves. And the riders are up for some fun as much as the punters. At the Railway Inn, which was taken over by Radio TT as one the broadcasting venues, riders like Martin Finnegan and Richard Britton came along to be interviewed, and spent more time playing Jenga than doing the PR bit. We all had a stab at the game which involves stacking small pieces of wood and then removing them one by one. The player who collapsed the pile was the loser. I heard one or two punters suggesting that you'd never find Premiership footballers doing anything like that. My experience is that you certainly would – only the footballers would be placing sizeable bets on the outcome.

The riders outdid themselves at the Villa on the Thursday of Practice Week. Along with the Department of Tourism, the riders' liaison officers Milky Quayle and Paul Phillips hosted *A Question of TT Sport*, featuring two teams of riders, with Milky asking the questions. Milky paraded from the back of the hall to take his seat on stage. From the front he was the dapper host – pressed shirt, bow tie, dark trousers. From the rear he was something else entirely – bare back, naked buttocks, and a nifty thong to cover his necessaries. Two teams of riders, captained by John McGuinness and Ian Lougher, grappled with Milky's questions (including: Who is the most recent Manxman to win a solo TT? Answer: M Quayle) but the house was brought down by the glamour girls who paraded the scores at the end of each round. Beneath fetching blonde wigs and skimpy bikinis were the less-than-feminine forms of Paul Owen and Robbie Silvester, both due to ride in the upcoming races. The sight of Paul flashing his legs at the assembled throng was enough to put you off sex for – well, for at least as long as it took to down a couple more pints.

It was brilliant entertainment, which must have been great for the riders too. It certainly took their minds off the hard graft that goes with the TT, with only one day's practice remaining before the start of the races.

The following day I watched practice at Ballaugh Bridge. It would be my last chance to see action away from the Grandstand. Finnegan was the star of the show. He launched his Honda over the hump-backed bridge like a Tornado fighter taking off from the deck of an aircraft carrier. He achieved so much more distance through the air than anyone else that he looked to be riding a totally different kind of machine. The next most spectacular was another Irish lad, David Coughlan. I'd encountered David sitting in a canvas chair inside his tent in the paddock earlier in the week. This was his TT debut and, like so many of the riders he'd taken time out from his 'proper' job in order to be here – in David's case, working as a joiner at a hotel in Cork. At 35, David was stepping up after a couple of campaigns in the Manx Grand Prix. He had the backing of a sponsor, Mike O'Brien, and from what I saw out at Ballaugh he was certainly giving it everything he had.

There were a lot of gaps in the paddock that year. The organisers had excluded 125s and 400s, and many riders had decided to call it a day. The number of absentees first hit me when I was updating my database from the previous year. Any rider who was not competing in 2005 was transferred to a separate file on my computer and when I totted up the numbers there were no fewer than 77 riders who hadn't crossed the Irish Sea this time. Some were absent for reasons of fitness, machinery and sponsorship problems, or other commitments, but the vast majority were riders who would normally have turned up. They included people like Steve Linsdell, a name associated with the TT throughout my years attending the races, with seven podiums to his credit. Garry Bennett, a regular aboard his 125 since 1993 was another who'd called it a day, and the absence of Robert Dunlop, five times a TT winner, meant that the Dunlop name was missing from the TT for the first time since 1975. In 1989, when Joey was absent, Robert took part, and had maintained the family connection since Joey's death in 2000.

Maria Costello was also missing. Maria and several other riders decided not to race because the axing of the Production races at the TT meant there was no longer an avenue for riders to enter the Production classes and still be eligible for the Manx GP. So we were deprived of the chance to watch the fastest woman ever around the Mountain Circuit, a title Maria had grabbed when she clocked 114.73mph before retiring in the Proddie 1000 in 2004. I checked Maria's intentions in an exchange of e-mails before that year's TT, and she assured me she intended to ride in the Manx. "And my aim now is to win!" she declared.

The paddock still contained its usual share of characters, though. Tucked away in a far corner I came across Robert Price, known officially in the Race Guide as Robert A Price. If there was a starker contrast from the superbly-kitted trucks and professional crews provided at the top end of the paddock I'm sorry I didn't find it, but here was Robert, accompanied by his aged collie dog Stanley, a fortnight away from his 57th birthday, taking time out from his job as a restorer of vintage cars, still as enthusiastic as ever about gunning his Suzuki GSXR 600 around the Manx roads (Robert, that is, not Stanley). Robert first came to the island for the Manx in 1983, stepped up to the TT two years later, twice took fourth place in the old Singles TT, and he did well enough this time to add a bronze replica to his trophy cabinet for his performance in the second of the two Supersport races.

Markus Barth had one of the smartest motorhomes, with bold red and black livery and all the internal trimmings. Markus, from Munich, was making his TT debut at the age of 33. "I've always wanted to do the TT, but I was never allowed to by my team, although I've raced seven times at Macau," he told me. "Now, I have my own team – so I can come!"

Markus seemed to have it all worked out. "I will ride for another two years, then I will run the team with two young riders," he said. "My aim is to have a podium finish at the TT in 2007." This time Markus' preparations were complicated by his commitments to ride in the BMW International Boxer Cup series. This meant he had to miss the final practice session, and couldn't enter the Superbike TT because he had to compete in the BMW series at Mugello. I bumped into him again after he flew back to the island and asked how it went. "Shit," was the blunt answer. "Brake problems, had to retire on the second lap." It was a long way for a big let-down.

Another member of the Continental contingent was Patrick van Gils, a Belgian who was usually to be found driving a monster crane which carried containers across the docks in Antwerp. Patrick's truck was almost as big as the crane. One of the most fascinating riders was Frenchman Marc Granié, 51 years of age and a motorcyclist by profession – but a different kind of biking. Marc worked for the French police as a member of the motorcycle escort team. "I've escorted the President of France, the Pope, and all sorts of foreign leaders," he told me. Marc, a former Army parachutist, had been coming to the TT since 1986, with a best placing of seventh aboard a Bimota in the 2000 Singles TT. He missed 2004 but had a good reason. "I had to work escorting VIPs at the 60th anniversary celebrations of the Normandy Landings," he said. Marc was due to ride a Voxan in the Senior. The French marque had first appeared the previous year, Fabrice Miguet the rider, and made a big impact with the lovely throaty roar of the engine. Marc was a fascinating character and easy to talk to despite the fact that he spoke virtually no English – he was one of those natural communicators who could hardly wait to share his enthusiasm for the sport. I knew that, like many others around the paddock, he wouldn't be up there among the podium finishers, but I would still keep an eye out to check how he got on.

Magnificent McGuinness

It's never pleasant to hear a fellow human being yelp with pain. It's even more disconcerting when that fellow human is your producer and you are live on air at the time!

It was the final day of racing at TT 2005 and the scouts were forming up on the track for the annual presentation of the trophy for the best troop. Now, I have to admit that the previous year I let the cat out of the bag by announcing the name of the top troop before the official announcement down below. I didn't know that it was supposed to be a surprise. This time I was aware of the situation so I wasn't going to make the same mistake again. Eunice Crossley – showing an alarming lack of confidence in her presenter – clearly thought I was about to put my foot in it again. I announced that the presentation was about to take place. "The trophy will go to ..." There was an anguished howl to my left and a pair of hands plonked themselves across the sheet of paper, preventing me from reading any more. "The trophy will go to," I continued as calmly as I could, "the troop which has performed best over the course of the TT and also the Manx Grand Prix." I looked round to see Eunice doubled up in some sort of contortion, and the rest of the personnel collapsing in various states of merriment. It was one of those moments when it was necessary to explain over the air what was going on behind the scenes because I couldn't stop laughing. I mustered as much dignity as I could, and rebuked my producer for her lack of faith. This time, at least, I was in possession of the moral high ground, so I thought I would make the most of it.

The race itself was another masterclass by John McGuinness who led from start to finish. It was a race of high attrition, with big names dropping out one by one – Paul Hunt retiring in the pits at the end of lap one, Adrian Archibald out at the Bungalow on lap two, Ryan Farquhar stopping at Parliament Square on lap three, and Raymond Porter also making a premature exit. At the halfway point McGuinness had a 23-second lead over Richard Britton, with Ian Lougher three seconds further back, and Guy Martin 11 seconds down on Lougher.

The second pit stop finished any chance Britton had of hauling in the leader. It also gave us one of the most memorable pieces of commentary of 2005. As Britton fired up the Honda, it was Chris Kinley who spotted that the chain wasn't properly looped up. "The chain's off the sprocket," bellowed Chris into his microphone, the live broadcast sending his words via the PA speakers all the way down pit lane. "The chain's off the sprocket, the chain's off the sprocket, tell him, tell him." Britton's crew was still trying to get him away. It seemed an age before the penny dropped and they got the chain fixed. Away went Richard, and into the broadcasting vaults went Chris' commentary. It was fantastic stuff – as live as live can be: instinctive, accurate and passionate. The other thing that gave these moments something extra was that we, the audience, actually knew a vital piece of information which the rider and his team didn't know. So Radio TT was putting our listeners one step ahead of the experts. TT fans logged in over the internet from New Zealand or South Africa knew what the problem was with Britton's Honda before the man who was riding the thing.

The incident immediately dropped Richard from second to fifth place which was where he finished, not the first piece of bad luck the man from Enniskillen had endured over the Mountain Course – and not his last either, because he was back later in 2005 to ride Brian Richards' Tickle Manx in the Junior Classic at the Manx Grand Prix. Awarded the same number eight as his TT rides in '05, Richard was forced to retire the bike at Sulby Bridge on lap two, but his mere presence added excitement to the MGP that year. Very sadly, it was to be Richard's last appearance on the Isle of Man as a crash at the Ballybunion road races on September 18th cost him his life. I first met him in the build-up to TT 2004, and was immediately impressed by how approachable and engaging he was. He was a talented rider who would surely have won a TT had he been granted more time.

Magnificent McGuinness duly sewed up the race to win by 34 seconds from Lougher, with Guy Martin the main beneficiary of Britton's trauma with the chain and sprocket. Guy moved up to third to clinch his first TT podium; a well deserved reward for his memorable contributions to the festival that year. Guy made his mark through the determined brilliance of his riding but also his perky presence all round the scene – from dressing as a boy scout for the 'feel a sportsman' round of Milky Quayle's quiz at the Villa, to giving Radio TT a series of searingly honest interviews; Guy was the talk of the island. He had to work for his podium – Martin Finnegan, starting 11 places ahead on the road, was also going for it good-style. When the stopwatches clicked for the final time Guy had done it by just one tenth of a second; breathless stuff!

It was a memorable Senior for Jun Maeda. When I spoke to the Japanese rider before Race Week – with the help of his interpreter – he told me his ambition was to clinch a top-ten finish. There was plenty of Japanese machinery on view, but Jun was the only Japanese rider involved. Jun had terrific enthusiasm for the TT. He was a worthy successor to the previous Japanese riders to compete at the TT dating back to 1959 and the first appearance of the famous Honda quartet, Naomi Taniguchi, Teisuke Tanaka, Giichi Suzuki and J Suzuki.

Jun told me the Fireblade was "... the best bike Honda has built," and as a freelance development rider whose CV included work on the 'Blade, he was in a position of authority. He came into the Senior in good form, having achieved his top ten aim with ninth place in the first superbike race, and followed up with ninth and sixth in the two Supersport races. Jun piloted his 'Blade to sixth place again, having moved into the top ten at Ramsey on lap two, and advanced steadily as riders dropped out up front. The Yorkshireman Ian Hutchinson capped a good TT by taking eighth place, realising the potential he showed when winning the 2003 Manx Grand Prix 750 Newcomers race in sensational style, and Nigel Beattie surprised himself by finishing ninth, a great effort on the big Yamaha superbike for the Laxey rider, whose main claim to fame at the TT was in the now-defunct 125 class. Chris Palmer, another 125 specialist forced to review his options in 2005, was another with reason to smile, taking tenth place.

By the time I left the commentary box I was aware there had been a serious accident on the far side of the course. Usually we get to know if there's been a crash which might prove fatal but we're not allowed to say anything about it until details have been confirmed and next-of-kin informed; only right and proper. I was told that a marshal had been killed in the Kirk Michael area but it wasn't until later that I learned that Cumbrian rider Gus Scott had also died in the same incident. I'd met Gus in the Hilton's Colours bar during Practice Week. He was a newcomer and couldn't wait to get the racing under way. He spent a long time talking to Andy McGladdery who, of course, knew the Mountain Course inside out from his racing days. The incident became one of the most controversial in the recent history of the TT when it transpired that the marshal, April Bolster, had been crossing the track and couldn't get out of the way when Gus came through. The fact that she was marshalling outside her house, in view of members of her family, made it even more horrific. It was a grim conclusion to the TT of 2005.

The Manx Motor Cycle Club regrets to announce

Death on the Mountain Course is a fact of racing. It would be lovely to think that, in the future, people won't die pursuing their sporting goals, but if history teaches us anything it is that every year at least one competitor will not be going home. 2005 was bad enough at the TT, with three fatal accidents costing the lives of Gus Scott, Swedish newcomer Joakim Karlsson, and sidecar driver Les Harah, but the Manx was even worse – six riders lost their lives.

The virtual certainty that riders will die is what makes racing on the Isle of Man such a challenge. It is the ultimate test of road racing in every way. The riders will tell you that they cope with the risks by riding just within themselves and not on the absolute edge – but when they're going for the chequered flag and there are only seconds in it, can they really abide by that? Probably not. But that doesn't tell the real story because the majority of fatal accidents do not happen to riders pushing for podium places. Machine failure is as likely to be to blame as rider error, and accidents can be caused by circumstances beyond the control of the riders or their crews, as the Gus Scott incident demonstrates. Many different factors cause fatal accidents, making it impossible for the organisers to come up with straightforward solutions.

Death does not distinguish between the fast and the slow, the experienced and the newcomers. It can take a maestro like David Jefferies as implacably as it can take a raw novice like Serge le Moal, the Frenchman who died before reaching Braddan Church on his very first practice lap in 2004. But while it is seldom a surprise, it is still always a shock. I wasn't involved in 2003 but I vividly remember where I was when I learned of DJ's death. I was reading the morning paper aboard a cross-channel ferry en route for Calais when the news caught my eye. I pushed the paper away in a reflex action, as if removing the source of the information would also remove its meaning. If only.

I interviewed Mark Farmer for BBC TV during Practice Week in 1994 when Mark was riding the Britton. He was all set to go, helmet on. He was killed before he could make it back. Two years later I rang the race office one morning in Practice Week to arrange an interview with Mick Lofthouse, one of the leading contenders from my *North West Tonight* patch. There was a horrible silence before I was quietly informed that Mick had been killed in early practice that morning. Three years on and I was waiting at Liverpool Airport to fly across when word came that another of the riders I knew, Simon Beck, had died the previous night.

There's no escaping the fact that this is a horrible state of affairs. The age of the Roman Colosseum is long gone. We don't go to sport to see people die. But on the Mountain Course it is inevitable. So it becomes a question of how we deal with it. And because it is inevitable, because it is a regular situation, the Isle of Man deals with it differently from anywhere else.

Rallying is a dangerous sport too, but fatal accidents are so unusual that when a competitor was killed at the Welsh Rally in 2005 it was national news and the stage was abandoned. Fellow drivers lined up in silence as a mark of respect before the rally resumed. At the TT there is none of that. Racing continues regardless. Flags are not lowered to half-mast. There is no minute's silence. And I'd noticed in previous years that the death of a rider was not even mentioned when Peter Kneale went through the Race Guide changes. The missing rider would simply be glossed over as a non-starter, as if he was suffering nothing worse than a misfiring engine. From the outside it seems unbelievably callous.

Callous is not the right word. Privately, and behind the scenes, people are as upset and concerned as you would expect of decent human beings, from the clerk of the course down. But there is no public demonstration of grief. Instead, the families and pit crew tidy things up and move out when they can. For days after Karlsson's death in practice in 2005 his tent stood forlorn in the paddock, a Swedish flag stuck under the awning. Then, suddenly, it was gone.

In the touchy-feely politically correct world that most of us inhabit, it all seems obscene. But really, what are the alternatives? Flags would spend too long at half-mast. Riders would observe a minute's silence too often. These are, after all, men and women who are themselves doing battle with their own fears. They know how risky it is. On race day they have to be clear of mind and strong of nerve. Weepy tributes are an indulgence no-one can afford at this event. And should the organisers do more in public than simply issue a press release that at that time always began with the words: "The Manx Motorcycle Club regrets to announce that a competitor was fatally injured ...?" I often felt they should, without quite knowing what. But if they spent too long reflecting on the latest fatality while racing was under way, would they have the stomach to carry on with the show at all? There is time afterwards to mourn, to conduct inquests, to mull over the safety implications.

The Isle of Man is not in that touchy-feely politically correct world that most of us inhabit the rest of the year. We are in a place where red-blooded challenges are still exactly that, where the penalties for failure are not watered down, where you survive if you're good enough and lucky enough, and may not survive at all if you are neither. That's the bargain, and you buy into it of your own choice. No-one races because they have to. They all race because they want to. And they all know every last paragraph of the bargain.

In 1999 I thought I was witnessing a TT fatality when Paul Orritt came off his Honda Firestorm right in front of my camera crew at the foot of Bray Hill. Paul was thrown heavily into an embankment on the left-hand side of the road and bounced back onto the tarmac. His bike went spinning up the road, almost taking out a marshal who was running towards the scene. The red flags came out and there was a lengthy hold-up before he could be transported away by ambulance. Thankfully, he lived, but was too battered to continue his racing career. Twelve months later, where was Paul Orritt? Back at the TT, spectating and supporting. I met him in Jak's Bar on Douglas Promenade, minus a few fingers and somewhat grumpy, but unable to resist the magnetism drawing him back to the TT.

It's the same with the fans. When I covered the TT for BBC TV I usually spent the last few days of Practice Week on the island, stayed for the opening race day and Mad Sunday, and flew back to Manchester on the Monday. One year I got back to Manchester to learn of a bad crash at Brandish in which a bike had shot over the steep banking on the outside of the bend (it was a sharper bend than it is now) and badly injured a young girl from Oxfordshire who was spectating there. The next day I flew straight back to put together a report. As you can imagine, everyone was distressed. But a year later, when I contacted the family to find out how she was, where were they? In the same holiday cottage in Foxdale, looking forward to another year at the races!

People who take on the TT know what they're letting themselves in for, which is why, in my opinion, they never turn on the event if something goes wrong. Quite the reverse. They usually talk about how much pleasure and camaraderie they've had on the island, the very comments made by the family of Geoff Sawyer after his death at the 2005 Manx Grand Prix.

From my perspective, however, as a broadcaster and journalist, the passing of a rider was not something to be glossed over by describing him as a 'non starter' when I read out the changes to the Race Guide over the airwaves. In my view, riders are due more respect. So I devised my own method of dealing with this tricky subject. If a rider had been killed I mentioned the fact and paid tribute to him the next time we introduced a race in which he should have competed. After the tragic death of Tommy Clucas in the Manx Grand Prix when leading the Junior race in 2004, I spoke some words of tribute during the build-up to the Senior race. A full year later his team boss, Martin Bullock, went out of his way to tell me how much the team had appreciated my words. That meant a lot. It isn't easy to get the words and the tone right. Clearly it's something I hoped I would never have to do again after Tommy, but all too often I did.

2006 – Under the baseball cap was the lap record holder

Tooth and nail

When I arrived on the island for the 2006 TT festival I soon discovered that the biggest grin belonged not to John McGuinness, Bruce Anstey or any of the top riders. It belonged, beyond all doubt, to Robbie Silvester.

Robbie, the Yorkshire rider who had spent most of the 1980s racing short circuits before trying his hand at rugby league and then coming late to road racing, was the proud owner of the most handsome set of gnashers since the extinction of the sabre-toothed tiger. "I've spent a grand on these," he told me when I ran into him at the Amber Lounge on Douglas Promenade, indicating a shiny top-set. "I got fed up of having chipped teeth thanks to all the bumps you get in this business. So I had them done last year. And this year," he added, "I'll be wearing a good-quality gumshield when I'm racing!"

The teeth were the good news. The bad news was that Robbie was still suffering from a broken shoulder sustained at Scarborough at the start of May. He'd been having laser treatment in Ipswich and hyperbaric treatment in Yorkshire. He'd managed to race at the North West 200 nine days after the spill, but hadn't felt fully competitive. And it quickly got worse. Robbie sustained various fractures in a spill at Greeba during Practice Week and, sadly, ended up with little to smile about in 2006 after all.

But at least he was here, which was more than could be said for a number of riders. I was surprised by the number of withdrawals through injury at non-TT events. Ryan Farquhar's absence was the most high-profile following a crash in practice at Cookstown in April. Also scratched were Ken Doherty, Kevin Mawdsley, Stefano Bonetti and Kenny McCrea, along with the Belgian rider Michael Weynand and Italian newcomer Angelo Conti.

In one motorhome I came across two lads who struck me as wishing they had scratched as well. Sidecar aces Tom Hanks and Phil Biggs were hardly full of the joys of spring, and that wasn't even partially explained by my visit coinciding with Tom being roused from the sleeping quarters. Hanks and Biggs were back at the TT after an absence of seven years. Most of the interim they had spent competing in the World Championships, finishing third in 2005. This year, lack of sponsorship had ruled them out of the Worlds, and they were clearly feeling somewhat left out – the 2006 series was starting over the same weekend as opening practice on the Mountain Course. They both seemed dubious at the prospect of risking life and limb at the TT. "If it doesn't feel right, I'll just pull in and that'll be it," said Tom, with Phil nodding in agreement. I told them they'd surely feel the old adrenalin kicking in once they got out on the track, but they didn't seem convinced.

Much more optimistic was another sidecar pilot, Greg Lambert. The Yorkshire engineer sounded like he meant business this time after a dismal time in 2005 – although his experience then did show what is so special about the TT: "In the first race we ran out of petrol at Windy Corner. An old feller came up and gave us fuel from a can which got us to the finish. Then in race two my visor was ripped off as we flew down Bray Hill on lap one. I stopped at Quarterbridge and shouted to the crowd: 'can anyone lend us a lid?' In no time I was being given dozens to choose from! I got fixed up and carried on, but eventually we had to retire in Parliament Square."

Greg and his partner Rick Long were looking forward to the action on the island before competing in the European F1 Championship, and then, if all went to plan, the World Championship in 2007.

Sidecar drivers are a breed apart. Even in the non-conformist, mould-breaking world of biking, the three-wheeled brigade are, well, different. Take the case of Dan Clark. Dan was competing in his fifth TT in 2006, at the age of 58. He'd come to the sport late, at the age of 44, following a bold New Year's resolution to take up sidecar driving. His wife heard him and, to his amazement, insisted he should fulfil the resolution. He took after his dad, Les, who began sidecar racing at the age of 55 and carried on till 67, partnered by Dan's mother Stella who only retired from chair duties after her 61st birthday.

What made the Clark setup even more remarkable was that Les was still racing with them, even though he'd been dead for six years. "He's in there," Dan told me, pointing to a black casket bolted inside the fairing. "Those are his ashes."

He explained, "Dad always used to come to races with us, especially Scarborough. He died in 2000, shortly before we were due to go to Oliver's Mount. After the funeral we took the ashes with us, scattered some there, and kept the rest with the bike. Now he comes with us in every race. Up to now we've finished every race we've taken part in here at the TT."

Dan, who was partnered in 2006 by Dave Clark, no relation, had an unnervingly down-to-earth attitude to his racing. No frills, no wild boasts, no hype. He just loved what he did. Take the Yamaha R6 engine he was installing. "I got this on eBay," he told me. "It cost me 99 quid." I thought he was pulling my leg, but no. It was true. "It didn't have a second gear, but that didn't matter because it came with a spare gearbox. We stripped it down, rebuilt it, and it's been fine. I bought two other R6 engines off eBay for £300 each. Three engines for less than £700! Not bad!"

And what did this advocate of the high risk lifestyle of the TT racer do for a living? He was a health and safety advisor for Calderdale Council! Do as I say, not as I do, must be his motto!

Most of the sidecar teams were unhappy with the organisers that year. The new racing schedule had moved the first Sidecar TT from the Saturday to the Monday, with the second race on the Wednesday. It meant they had only one day between races, instead of three. That would have a huge impact on their ability to rebuild engines and sort all the other problems race one would inevitably produce. It also meant there was no practice time for them to try out any changes. I had complete sympathy with them. I couldn't see how moving the first race back to the Monday helped anyone. I felt it reduced the spectacle of the opening day of the TT races. To have the superbikes and the sidecars out on day one was a fabulous way to start the proceedings. This year, it was not to be and I could well understand the disappointment of the three-wheeled brigade.

Bad crashes and new talent

The racing schedule for 2006 was a real puzzle. The organisers reduced the number of solo races from five to four. It was one heck of a contrast from my first year as anchor when there were seven solo races, two of them run concurrently. In 2004 John McGuinness had six opportunities to win. In 2006 he had only four. There was controversy, too, about the introduction of a new TT licence all competitors had to have. The stipulations included a requirement that each competitor must have taken part in at least three road races between July 2005 and March 2006. A number of riders thought this was unfair, especially those who had missed significant racing time through injury.

Chris Heath, the Baldrine rider who'd been competing for ten years and boasted eighth place at the inaugural Superbike TT, explained that, in order to rack up the minimum number of races, he had travelled to

Pembrey in South Wales in March, then straight back to the Isle of Man to race at Jurby the next day. "That doesn't seem the safest way to go about things," he said. "At Pembrey I couldn't risk racing properly. I just had to make sure I finished."

Even so, it was understandable that the organisers should tighten entry requirements. Whatever formula they came up with was never going to satisfy everyone, but the TT is such a dangerous event that some check on riders' current form was no bad thing.

Practice week gave everyone a severe reminder of the risks. On the Monday evening Jun Maeda, the sole Japanese competitor for many years, suffered fatal injuries in an incident involving Seamus Greene on the Ballahutchen Straight coming out of Union Mills. Maeda was airlifted to hospital in Manchester but died the following week. It was horribly ironic. Minutes before the accident he had been feted by the Mayor of Tokyo who was visiting the TT that day with an entourage of VIPs and media. In honour of the occasion Jun had been allowed to lead off the practice session amid much publicity. It all seemed too cruel.

Then, on the Thursday, Dave Molyneux and his passenger Craig Hallam, replacing Dan Sayle in the chair, were lucky to survive a 140mph crash on the exit from Rhencullen. Their outfit tipped over backwards, pinning Moly underneath, before sliding to a halt and bursting into flames. It was the end of Moly and Craig's TT campaign. Thankfully it was not the end of Moly and Craig.

That crash rammed home another of the risks that competitors at the TT run – the financial variety. Moly had sunk thousands of pounds and heaven knows how many man-hours into preparing for the TT, knowing that he stood to earn several thousand pounds by winning the two races. At a stroke, that income was wiped out. Then there was the cost of repairing or replacing his bike so he could get back onto the racing scene in the future. And his injuries meant that earning his normal living would be tricky for the next few weeks, even if Dave did surprise everyone by leaving hospital the very next day and appearing at the TT Riders Chat Show at the Villa Marina, to a thunderous reception.

David Bell didn't crash quite so spectacularly as Moly but the outcome was much the same. Dave came off at Greeba in Thursday practice, crashing into air fencing which had been torn out of position by Robbie Silvester's crash moments earlier, and breaking his wrist. Again, all the months of preparation and planning went out of the window. The Chester-le-Street rider had backing from Newcastle Kawasaki for all four solo races, and, after a disappointing 2005, he was looking to build on a very promising ninth place in the Senior on his debut year, 2004. Sadly, it was not to be. Dave's wife Susan and four-month-old son Spencer were there to cheer him up, and it was good to see Dave sticking around throughout Race Week to support the other riders.

On a somewhat less serious note, I woke up on the day of our first live broadcast, the Thursday of Practice Week, to the commentator's worst nightmare. Blocked nose, runny eyes, the shivers, and a throat which felt like the inside of the exhaust can on McGuinness' Honda. It was the last thing I needed before embarking on hours of unpredictable live commentary.

A commentator with no voice is like a rider with no bike: useless. It had never afflicted me before, although, on one memorable occasion, I was the surprise beneficiary when someone else was struck dumb. That was at the Commonwealth Games in Manchester in 2002 when John Rawling, one of the BBC's top commentators, lost his voice while covering the track and field. John was also due to cover the finals of the boxing but had to step aside. I was working as boxing reporter for the BBC during the games, filing live updates on the preliminary rounds. Suddenly, I was pitched in as commentator for the finals. It was great! Just what a sports broadcaster loves, to be at the heart of dramatic, live action.

So now I faced a battle to be fit for the start of racing in 24 hours' time. I decided to tackle each symptom individually, so I hit the pharmacies and health shops, hoovering up a selection of tablets and potions to tackle the throat, the head, the eyes, and to rebuild the body's natural resistance and restore some energy. When I'd been on holiday in Cyprus I bought a pot of vile yellow squirty liquid which was brilliant for a sore throat then. I still had some left so it came into play once again. My wife Dorothy, who is skilled in a number of complementary therapies, arrived from England that day and gave me an M-technique massage. We spent the afternoon on Laxey beach, in glorious sunshine, letting nature do its bit. "Soak up those negative ions," commanded Dorothy. I soaked as many as I could.

I don't know which bits worked but come race day I was feeling a lot better. The voice felt and sounded pretty gruff, but at least it was functioning. And it was a day no-one would have wanted to miss, thanks to John McGuinness.

With eight TT wins under his belt John was the clear pre-race favourite in the TT Superbike event. But it was Ian Hutchinson who led on adjusted time as they passed Maurice Mawdsley at Glen Helen on lap one. Ian was to make a big impact at TT 2006, but in this opening race his time at the top of the leader board was shortlived. McGuinness was 12 seconds ahead of Ian when they passed us at the Grandstand at the end of the first lap, and stayed in front to the end. But that's only part of the story. This was one incredible performance by McGuinness and the

HM Plant Honda team. From a standing start he demolished his own lap record on the opening lap, the time of 17 minutes 42.52 flashing up on my computer, a speed of 127.835mph, improving on his 2004 record of 127.68. Lap two was even better. Despite slowing for the pit stop, John clocked 17 minutes 41.71, a speed of 127.933mph. Clearly the first 128mph lap was on the cards. By the end of six laps he had racked up his ninth TT win and claimed a race record, one hour 48 minutes 52.06 seconds, 39 seconds ahead of second-placed Ian Lougher. It was Honda's first win in the opening big-bike event since Joey Dunlop in 2000.

And the race gave us a lot more. It signalled that Ian Hutchinson and Cameron Donald were now names to be reckoned with around the Mountain Course. Hutchy, a protégé of David Jefferies, and, like DJ, a Yorkshireman, held second place at the first pit stop and thereafter looked very comfortable in third as he clinched his first TT podium. Equipped with a Kawasaki ZX10 supplied by the McAdoo racing team, Hutchy confirmed the rich promise he'd shown at the Manx Grand Prix in 2003 when he won the 750 Newcomers race on a Honda CBR600, becoming the fastest newcomer to lap the course at either the MGP or TT. At the age of 26, this self-employed mechanic from Bingley was making a very strong statement about the future of the TT.

And Cameron Donald, the 27-year-old from Melbourne, Australia, was another who proved that the TT was still a magnet for up-and-coming racers. Cameron was here as a spectator in 2004, made his debut in 2005 backed by MGP rider Mick Charnock, and now, riding for Uel Duncan's team on a Honda Fireblade, took a very impressive fifth place. TT 2006 had put its troubles behind it and was off to an exhilarating start!

The slowest and the fastest

"Maybe," I pondered on air during a quiet moment in the commentary box, "there should be an award for the *slowest* person to arrive at the Isle of Man for the TT." Not a serious suggestion – but there again, at the TT you never know! – it was prompted by bumping into two diehard spectators just before I entered the tower for the day's broadcasting. Lawrence Cross and Chas Heath had taken over a month to reach the island – and they'd only been coming from Yorkshire! It turned out that the two of them, as well as being bike fans, were also narrowboat enthusiasts. They had departed from Doncaster on the canal network on April 20th and cruised westwards to Lancaster before completing the trip by Steam Packet from Heysham. "What is your narrowboat called?" I asked Chas. "Rhencullen!" came the reply. Why was I not surprised?!

The TT fortnight is about the spectators as much as the competitors. An even more remarkable duo were Barry Birdsall and his son John, from Derbyshire. John suffers from a serious disability but that had not prevented him from turning into a real action-man, piloting his motorised wheelchair – officially a 'Nippy' powerchair – all round the country, and undertaking daredevil activities like skydiving. The family had been in contact with a firm from Greater Manchester, Martin Conquest, which had just unveiled a spectacular-looking trike designed to give bikers with disabilities the freedom to ride the roads without having to be lifted off their wheelchairs. The Conquest machine allowed the rider to drive the wheelchair up an electronically-lowered ramp, anchor it inside the trike, and operate all the controls by hand. The engine was based on the BMW R series, and had the vital bonus of a reverse gear. It claimed 0-60mph in 8.6 seconds, a top speed of 107mph, max power of 83bhp at 6750rpm, and was on sale at £21,495. Barry had been given the chance to bring the trike to the island where I spotted him cruising cheerfully along outside the Gaiety Theatre, with John in close company. I tracked them down to the Hilton Hotel and caught up with their exploits. The Conquest trike made a big impact, and it spoke volumes for the pulling power of the TT that the manufacturer had despatched it to the island to raise its profile.

Meanwhile, the times when the TT anchor predicts a race winner accurately are few and far between! So I make no apology for gloating, even after all this time, over forecasting in our pre-race build-up that Bruce Anstey would win the 2006 TT Superstock on the Monday.

This was not such a clear call as it looks in hindsight. Anstey had retired at Crosby with clutch trouble on the first lap of the Superbike TT, and his TAS Suzuki team was in a spot of bother. Not only was it finding it difficult to win races, it was finding it difficult to get the bikes to the finish. Anstey's team-mate Adrian Archibald had retired after lap one on Saturday, and had also failed to finish his last two races in 2005, as indeed had Anstey. It all meant that no TAS bike had finished a TT in the last six attempts. But I had a feeling that Anstey, with his pedigree on the superstock machine, would come good this day, and so it proved. The Kiwi led almost from start to finish, although Ian Hutchinson started lap three dead level after a quick pit stop, and nosed briefly into the lead at Ramsey. Anstey, though, took control to win by 8.3 seconds for his fifth TT triumph on the tenth anniversary of his debut, and Suzuki's 40th TT success. Jason Griffiths was third.

John McGuinness settled for fifth place, but come the 600cc Junior TT it was business as usual. I'd happened across John and Hutchy on Douglas promenade the previous day. It was somewhat embarrassing. There I was, walking along after a pleasant lunch, and this character in a baseball cap suddenly appeared in front of me, dodging from side-to-side to prevent me going past. I was about to give him a volley of abuse when I realised that under the baseball cap was the lap record holder of the Isle of Man TT himself! Both lads were on fine form, enjoying a few hours off, taking in the sunshine and the fairground buzz. We chatted about the prospects for the Junior and John grabbed the opportunity to remind me that, even though the race magazines gave Ryan Farquhar as the lap record holder, it was in fact John McGuinness who was quickest on a 600. Ryan of course was credited with the lap record for the recently-introduced Supersport class, but his best speed of 122.64mph was inferior to John's 122.87mph set on the Yamaha R6 in 2004. It showed how seriously lap records matter, and rightly so. John is one of nature's nice guys, but he was not going to let anyone mistake where the limelight lay.

After the 2006 race, there was no excuse for anyone to make a mistake. John did it again: a new record from a standing start on lap one, which took the speed through the 123mph mark, and a higher speed still on lap two: 123.975mph. This was racing at its best – not only by John, but by Hutchy on the ZX6 and Anstey on the GSXR600. All three shredded the old lap record on the fourth and final lap when Hutchy's speed of 123.513 was only one thousandth of a second slower than McGuinness, while Anstey clocked 123.084. John joined the TT immortals by winning for the tenth time, on the same level now as Giacomo Agostini and Stanley Woods.

There was a sting in the tail. After the garlanding was done and the dust had settled, post-race scrutineering revealed that Hutchy's bike was illegal. Illegal by a hair's breadth, but that was enough to disqualify him. The problem arose when the inspectors found the exhaust camshaft lift was 0.22mm over the maximum permitted. All concerned stressed that no-one had been trying to take advantage and that the excess would not have contributed any boost in performance, but a distraught Hutchy was nevertheless ruled out, and so Anstey inherited runners-up spot with Jason Griffiths now third.

There were dark rumours that Hutchy would boycott the Senior TT, but happily, come Friday, he was on the grid as scheduled. It turned out that he didn't get very far, retiring at Ramsey on the first lap, and it was McGuinness' day once again. John smashed the 128 barrier on lap one, 128.146 his average speed as he passed the Grandstand. Then, in the re-run of his TT Superbike performance, he coaxed even more pace out of the Honda, 129.451 his latest outright lap record as he slowed into the pits at the end of lap two. After that it was race over as McGuinness buttoned up his 11th TT in style. But once again there was a lot more going on. Cameron Donald produced another barnstorming display to take second place, including a lap of 128.445mph on lap two, and Bruce Anstey's brutal determination saw him follow McGuinness through the 129 barrier for a final lap average of 129.045. It was thrilling stuff in perfect weather conditions. And from the commentator's point of view, it was everything you wanted – glorious weather, record breaking speeds, no serious accidents, a quality winner and the emergence of new hopes for the future. I suppose the only element missing was a genuinely tight finish. There's nothing better than the result still being in doubt right at the end, but when we'd witnessed motorsport of such exceptional quality it would have been greedy to complain. The moment when the 129 barrier fell in front of my very eyes was pure adrenalin – and that was in the sanctuary of the commentary box!

Three legs, three wheels, three wins!

"Three legs. Three wheels. Three wins for the Isle of Man duo!" That was my comment as Nicky Crowe and Darren Hope secured their third TT victory to wrap up the Sidecar Programme at TT 2006. The *Isle of Man Examiner's* special TT edition picked up the comment and led their report with it the following day. It would take more than that spectacular accident involving Dave Molyneux to prevent the host nation from dominating the sidecar races as usual.

Crowe and Hope won both races, which meant we had to look back eight races to find the last non-Manx win, by England's Ian Bell and Neil Carpenter in race 'A' in 2003. Nicky and Darren had prepared for the races with a kind of grim determination, little suspecting what glory lay in store. The talk in the build-up was how they would respond after a nasty crash at Scarborough a month ahead of the TT, in which the bike was badly damaged and Nicky broke his hand. The lads pulled out of their final practice right at the start of the lap, but come the first race there was no holding them. They didn't quite lead from start to finish – Steve Norbury was quickest at both Glen Helen and Ramsey on lap one before Crowe got into his stride. But then on lap two the local heroes became the second crew after Moly and Sayle to break the 20-minute lap: 19 minutes 55.97 seconds.

The one-two-three seemed well established as they raced down the west side of the island on the last lap: Crowe leading Norbury, with Simon Neary and Stuart Bond third. But then the telltale transponders relayed worrying news: no sign of Neary at Cronk ny Mona. Crowe crossed the line to take the win, Norbury took second, then it was John Holden who emerged in third place. It was some time before we heard from race control that Neary and Bond had crashed at Brandywell and been helicoptered to hospital. They were not in danger, but for a while the silence was intensely worrying.

Race 'B' was another Crowe/Hope triumph, with Steve Norbury again second and Roy Hanks a popular third. Not for the first time the

TT showed its capacity to come up with a good story. There is no greater supporter of the event than Roy. 2006 was the 40th anniversary of Roy's debut as a TT competitor. Think of that: the last time there was a TT minus Roy Hanks, the likes of Hailwood, Ago and Jim Redman were on the starting sheets, while England's footballers had yet to win the World Cup! A stalwart of the TT Supporters Club, Birmingham-based Roy even came to the island in the year of the foot and mouth crisis, to man the Supporters shop. In 1997 he won, and now here he was, back on the podium at the age of 58.

2006 was a fabulous TT. Wonderful weather, great racing, and a reduction in serious accidents. And the last of those was really important. The fatal accidents in the recent past had attracted a fair amount of media attention, not least from *Motorcycle News*. I've always been interested in how the media covers controversial events like the TT. I've been part of the system myself for long enough, and these days I spend a lot of time teaching the upcoming generation how to work in the media. So I followed with particular interest two investigations by *MCN* into the standard of marshalling at the TT.

MCN set the ball rolling in 2005 when it had two reporters sign on, unidentified, as marshals. Their undercover report exposed a number of shortcomings, and was, I felt, a good example of the media doing its job.

To their credit, the race authorities – the Department of Tourism, the Manx Motorcycle Club and the TT Marshals Association – took the comments on board. By the start of the 2006 festival the setup was better organised, better resourced, and training was more comprehensive. So it came as a surprise when *MCN* returned to the attack. Once again it infiltrated two reporters into the marshalling setup, and once again a highly critical report appeared in the paper. This time, in my judgement, *MCN* overstepped the mark. Many of the accusations made second time round seemed petty and irrelevant. One of the reporters thought it was dreadful that he, as a novice, was being sent out to work as part of a marshalling team on the course. He wasn't experienced enough to deal with any problems, he said. Well, of course he wasn't. That's why he was sent out as part of a larger group: to watch and learn. How did he think a rookie marshal would ever gain experience unless he/she were sent out to work?

MCN's second assault did no-one any favours, least of all itself. 'Boycott *MCN*' banners were reported at places around the circuit. And the ill-judged 2006 'expose' only undermined the effectiveness of the original investigation. Worse, the publicity risked damaging a very important part of marshalling: the need to keep recruiting. This consistently negative publicity could only undermine the morale of the marshals and deter would-be volunteers from signing up. It was for that reason that I made a point of addressing the issue over the air during commentary. I didn't particularly enjoy criticising fellow journalists, but this time *MCN* had got it wrong and I said so.

It wasn't just my opinion. Time after time, riders had come in after practice or racing to report how effective the marshalling was in 2006. It was, as I suggested on air, the opinions of the riders which mattered most. Significantly, *MCN* became very supportive of the races over the next few years.

As a footnote to the dramatic events of 2006, the island managed to excel itself before the year was out. I mentioned in the previous chapter that the one element lacking was a genuinely tight finish. We got that three months later at the Manx Grand Prix. I have never commentated on an event which produced such an extraordinary, dramatic and unforgettable climax as the Junior MGP that year, won by Yorkshireman Craig Atkinson (plate two) by one hundredth of a second from Ireland's Derek Brien (plate one). What gave the moment its impact was that the two riders had left the start line side-by-side, something that can never happen these days. At the Manx then, unlike the TT, riders set off in pairs, so we had 150 miles of full-on, wheel-to-wheel racing, with never more than two seconds between them. After three laps the gap was a mere seven-tenths of a second. At Cronk ny Mona on the final lap Atkinson had the lead but it was too close to call. They rocketed into view along Glencrutchery Road side-by-side. As they reached the line I shouted "Two!" into the microphone. Craig had nicked it. The computer told me how tight it was: 0.01 seconds. The closest finish in the history of the Mountain Course. It was a privilege to be the commentator who described it.

2007 – Even the UK press gave the TT a pat on the back

Delight and despair

No discussion of the Centenary TT of 2007 should start without recognising that this was the TT at which two members of the public lost their lives while doing nothing more dangerous than standing at the side of the road, watching.

The news reached us in the commentary box shortly after we'd enjoyed the sight of John McGuinness celebrating victory and the first 130mph lap. Delight turned to despair in less time than it takes for a cloud to pass across the face of the sun. Tim Glover, Manx Radio's sports editor, walked in and said: "Right, this information doesn't go out of this box until we get official clearance, but there's a bad accident at the 26th Milestone. One rider is dead and it looks like two spectators at least have died as well." At that stage we didn't know that the rider was Marc Ramsbotham, a newcomer who was well known to Chris Kinley. Marc had taken a tumble in practice and been advised to take plenty of hot baths to aid his recovery. He'd been calling in to Chris' house for his baths. As the news of his identity came out, Chris and his partner Emma were hit hard. But Chris still had to carry on with his job – there was still the centenary parade to come, then the formal presentation of trophies and replicas which Chris was obliged to host (and he did, in his usual uplifting style).

Of course, Marc's family was devastated. The news was broken in the official area at the top of the tower, which entailed what must have been an agonising traipse up all those steps to receive the news, and an equally horrendous descent afterwards. My wife Dorothy happened to be there as they came back down. "The steps aren't wide enough for two people to come down anything other than one by one," she told me. "So at the very time they needed to be close, Marc's wife, children and father had to come all the way down in single file."

Not long afterwards, though, Dorothy noticed another family group going up the steps – bounding up, wreathed in smiles, off to have their photos taken on the roof. Somehow that summed up the extremes of emotion that we see in few places other than the TT.

The deaths of the two spectators came as a stunning blow. It was the first time anyone had died watching the TT. That is itself a surprising statistic given the hazards of spectating, but it was no consolation to the families of Dean Jacob and Greg Kenzig, or the onlookers who were traumatised by what they witnessed up at the 26th Milestone.

As soon as we received clearance from the Clerk of the Course we made an announcement about the crash. I handed over to Tim who read the official statement. It included the fact that fatalities had occurred, without naming names at this stage. When Tim finished it was back to me to pick up and carry on. Not an easy task under the circumstances. It reminded me of the time during the Falklands War when I'd been presenting an evening sport-and-music show on Radio Merseyside and someone came in from the newsroom and said: "You'd better announce this." "This," printed off from the teleprinter, was the news that HMS Sheffield had been hit by an Argentine exocet missile and was sinking in the South Atlantic. With the image of men fighting for their lives in freezing waters, how do you get back to merry music and the latest release from Rod Stewart?

When I returned to England the week following the TT, everyone I spoke to immediately mentioned the fatal accident. That, I am sure, is exactly the reaction TT aficionados dreaded. But it was entirely justified. People were quite right to highlight it. They were quite right to give the accident higher priority than the breaking of records and the winning of races. Of course they were. If you are not horrified at the thought of people being killed while watching a sporting event, then you should perhaps question your own humanity.

Placing it in context is something that should only come later. And the context is that motorsport is, as it says on the tin, dangerous. That goes for spectators as well as participants. Things will inevitably go wrong from time to time, and sometimes the consequences can be beyond anyone's control. It was remarkable that no bystander had been killed before, given that a motorbike going out of control at over 100mph can wreak immense havoc. At the same TT, Paul Owen's chain snapped on the ultra-quick Sulby Straight. As it happened the chain snaked off the sprocket – but the rear wheel could have locked up if it had snagged. Where would the bike have ended up?

TT spectators as a breed had led a charmed life until 2007, but that was when their luck ran out. Over the course of a century it has still been safer, statistically, to watch the TT races than to watch big-time football or motor car racing. Small consolation on the day of the 2007 Senior TT, but worth remembering when assessing the long-term response.

From Collier to McGuinness

On the Tuesday of Practice Week 2007 I was sitting with my pal Hassan Patel, owner of Chillis restaurant at the north end of Douglas Promenade. Hassan is usually the most cheerful of people but this night he was really down. "TT centenary," he said with a shake of the head. "It's just nothing. All hype and nothing happening."

I was surprised. The previous day I'd been to an enjoyable re-enactment of the 1907 TT at St John's. I'd also popped into the Gaiety Theatre to view the trophies, and spent a few hours at a fascinating display of TT history at the Manx Museum. The weather was reasonable and practice was going well. But clearly that wasn't the mood on the streets. "Look out of the window," said Hassan. "How would you know there's a centenary going on?" He had a point. Driving down the prom, there was nothing to tell you anything out of the ordinary was happening. Where were the flags and banners proclaiming the great event? Why were the lampposts still draped in last year's tourist pennants? Surely the Isle of Man hadn't messed up, now of all times?

Ten days later, back in Chillis, the staff were working their socks off and Hassan was wreathed in smiles. Things had turned out well after all. Bunting on the lampposts? Who would have noticed if it had been there? Once Practice Week got into its stride, there were so many bikes and bike fans that no-one could have missed the fact that here was something really special. Chillis Restaurant even became a home from home for German rider Frank Spenner and his crew, who were sponsored by Hassan and carried his logo on the bike in return for a plentiful supply of excellent curries and rooms upstairs.

The Centenary TT was always going to struggle to match expectations – but it succeeded wonderfully. The racing was brilliant, history was made with the breaking of the 130mph barrier by John McGuinness, the turn-out of ex-stars and historic machines was breathtaking, the public turned up in droves, and the weather in Race Week was simply idyllic. Even the UK press gave the TT a pat on the back. Helped by proactive tactics from Simon Crellin, the TT's press officer, a procession of feature writers arrived on the island and duly filed positive despatches.

I was chuffed to be the anchorman at the time of the centenary, and thrilled to be able to describe the appearance of so many people who are part of the TT story as well as being heroes of my own sporting life: Carl Fogarty, John Surtees, Murray Walker. I'd given a lot of thought as to how to pitch the commentaries in this year of all years. I didn't want everything to be submerged in a morass of nostalgia – when the Radio TT music presenters handed over to me, it was for a description of the events of 2007, not a history lesson. Equally, I was aware that these events of 2007 were being viewed by everyone through a glass that stretched back a hundred years to the Edwardian era. So a degree of historical referencing was important, so long as it didn't dominate. I hope I got the mix right. My opening remarks when we went on air on the opening race day attempted to set the upcoming races in context:

"It all started 100 years ago – one hundred years and five days to be precise, when 25 bold adventurers set off from St John's on May 28th 1907. Little did they know what perils and glories lay ahead for them or the event; much has changed since then, much has not. The course still uses some of that original route, the stretch from Ballacraine to Kirk Michael, the Triumph motorcycle was represented then as it still is now, and the winner of the TT is still a rider who gains instant immortality.

"From Charles Collier and Rem Fowler, winners in 1907, to John McGuinness and Bruce Anstey, winners in 2006, it's been one heck of a motorcycling adventure. And now for the centenary races, now for the next piece of history."

I don't script much in my commentaries, but there are times when it's so important to get the words right – at the very least, to avoid daft slips. Therefore, I always script my introduction, even if it's only 30 seconds long. There's nothing worse than getting a live broadcast off to a bad start, and a well-constructed opening at least ensures we start as we mean to go on.

From that moment on, of course, anything can happen!

On that day, though, nothing much did. We went on air as usual at 9.45am, but the weather was far from promising. Even so, the bikes were out on Glencrutchery Road when it was announced that there would be a 30-minute delay as a result of an oil spill at the Bungalow. The oil was cleared up but while we were waiting the weather deteriorated and Neil Hanson called off the day's racing programme. The forecast for the Sunday was even worse, so the wait before we could begin the hundred-year celebration was frustratingly extended. The paddock buzzed with rumours that Honda had forced the issue once it had been discovered that regulations prevented hand-cutting slick tyres to help cope with a damp track, but both Honda and Neil Hanson brusquely denied the charge. It was desperate luck for many visitors who had to go home over the weekend and would depart without seeing any racing action. But it couldn't be helped.

We cheered ourselves up by spending the evening with the Martin

Bullock team at its base in the paddock. It was an eerie sensation walking through the paddock to reach Martin's base. A few hours earlier it was buzzing with people, bikes and gossip. Now it was like a ghost town – awnings zipped up, displays closed. The only buzz, predictably, was beneath the black and yellow canvas of the MBR team, where we made the very welcome acquaintance of Etienne Godart and his special brew.

I'd already downed a couple of bottles of Spitfire when Etienne, who had backing from the Bullock team for his 2007 rides, appeared on the scene. Wearing a beret and carrying an interesting-looking barrel under his arm, he looked like an extra from 'Allo 'Allo. Inside the barrel was a wine which, he explained, he made from the last pressings of the grape mixed with cognac. It was beautiful, really smooth and full of flavour. Martin's rider Ian Pattinson was making dire warnings about its capacity to blow our heads off, but I have to report that despite taking on board a fair amount of this particular French import I awoke next day feeling better than I had all week! They should dispense it on the NHS. Etienne was taking time out from running his chicken farm in the Dordogne. He had 30,000 birds on his premises. He also had three ostriches which he kept as pets. He was looking to sell up, he told me, so a few days later, in a quietish moment, I mentioned live on air that if anyone wanted to buy a chicken farm in the South of France, Etienne was the man, Chris Kinley instantly responded that Paul Bird (boss of the Stobart Honda team) might be keen. I thought Chris was having a laugh until he told me that Paul really was a chicken farmer. If a deal had gone ahead, I should have been on at least ten per cent, I reckoned. I'd have bought the place just for Etienne's wine.

The Manx Radio team for 2007 was unchanged from the previous year, in terms of the commentary line-up – the first year since I'd started when there hadn't been at least one change. Roy Moore had been handed the Ramsey gig in his own right in 2006. I felt the team had settled down really well. Everyone brought their own expertise and character to the commentaries, including the translators, Mavis Brown and Heike Perry. We all supported each other, and no-one was on an ego trip. But there was one highly significant addition to the raceday squad: Geoff Cannell was back, conducting post-race interviews with the top three riders in the media conference. Radio TT also used Geoff extensively during other periods, appearing on Charlie Williams' chat show and broadcasting reports on the practice sessions. He had actually made his return to Manx Radio at the Manx GP the previous year, conducting post-race interviews in the same way as TT 2007. Anthony Pugh had been thoughtful enough to ask if I would have any objection to Geoff being invited to take on this role. I had no objection at all – it was good that Geoff, so much a part of TT history himself, should be involved. I was pleased that Geoff himself was happy to take part; at least we were both batting for the same side.

"Switch off your brain and go for it!"

I mentioned in the previous chapter that I didn't script many of the thousands of words I had to produce during the course of a day-long stint in the commentary box. I also stated that the reason for scripting anything at all was to ensure things sounded good when it really mattered. Well, that's the theory! Listening back to Radio TT's coverage of the Senior in 2007, I realised I had made the most absurd cock-up. In the final countdown to the start of the race I recalled the early winners, "Charles Collier on a Matchless and Rem Fowler on a Honda." Honda! Some four decades before the company had even been founded? I haven't a clue where that came from – or why, considering I had my script in front of me which clearly stated "Rem Fowler, Norton." I must have been unconsciously following Guy Martin's TT philosophy as expressed to Chris Kinley: "Stick your thumb up your arse, switch off your brain, and go for it." Still, in over six hours of broadcasting, that was about the only slip, and I came away from the Centenary TT feeling reasonably happy with the way things had gone. I made a point of listening back to the recordings of the final day's racing, to review how things went, particularly my own performance, and, in 2007, I couldn't find too many reasons to give myself a kicking.

Things didn't always go smoothly. Take the problem with the garlands, for example. Ever since I started the anchorman job, and for years beforehand, the garlanding ceremony involved the formal presentation of a garland to each of the top three riders on the podium. It is, indeed, referred to as the *garlanding* ceremony. Well, in 2007 it wasn't quite like that. Mick Grant, seven-times a TT winner, was the honoured guest due to hand out the garlands at the end of the first race, the Superbike TT. As usual I called for the fanfare and the podium party made its way up the spiral staircase. It was my job to orchestrate the ceremony, and I duly called for appreciation for the rider in third place, Ian Hutchinson, and waited for Mick to hand over the garland. There was much fidgeting on the podium and nothing much seemed to be occurring. Ian was presented with his cap for third place and Mick shuffled across to where Guy Martin was standing as runner-up. I went through the ritual. Still no garland. Mick was looking helpless and shrugged to the crowd. On to the winner: John McGuinness. Thank goodness a garland appeared this time. For some reason the authorities must have decided to award a garland to the winner only. It was all a bit feeble – being presented with a baseball cap didn't seem much reward for the riders who'd battled through to second and third places. And no-one had thought fit to tell me about the change of policy, which made it all acutely embarrassing. "There must have been a serious failure of the garland harvest on the island this year," said someone from the back of the commentary box.

The race eventually started on the Monday morning, with Monday's schedule switching to the Tuesday. Even now there was another delay – two hours this time while we waited for cloud to lift. It was during this hold-up, while we were off the air, that Eunice Cubbon caught my eye and nodded towards my right-hand side. I turned round, and there was the outright record holder himself – John McGuinness. "So this is what goes on in here," he said, looking round our less-than-palatial surroundings. We weren't entirely sure how John had got into the tower, which has strictly controlled access even to superstars, but it was great to see him – especially when he showed such a keen interest in our broadcasting. "Your man at Glen Helen, Maurice Mawdsley," he said. "I've been listening to him for years but I wouldn't know him if I fell over him. His voice is so familiar and I'd love to meet him some time." We couldn't beam up Maurice from Glen Helen then and there, but we did the next best thing. I motioned Eunice to hand John headphones and a microphone and press the switch that linked her desk with Glen Helen. She did so and a stunned Maurice heard the voice of the then 11-time TT winner coming over the wire. They had a great chat. It made Maurice's day.

It's quite rare, in my experience, for a top sports competitor to show any interest in the way we the media transmit their deeds to the public. That's no criticism: there's no reason why they should have any greater interest than I have in, say, the way the ice cream gets to the salesman's van. But it makes it all the more rewarding when someone does take an interest. I recall Dave Bassett, then the manager of Wimbledon FC, asking a lot of pertinent questions when we were on the same table at a football awards do, but he, and now McGuinness, are the exceptions. Even when footballers retire and take up media work, they rarely have any desire to know what really goes on beyond the microphone.

John was in no hurry to move on. It was a good way of killing time where no-one could find him. "If it stays wet I won't win this," he said. "I'm not great in the damp. I'll be sixth or seventh." He also had some interesting comments to make about the riders who finish second and third. "Never get enough credit," he said. "It's always about the winner, but whoever finishes second and third deserve a lot of respect as well. They shouldn't be ignored." Garlands? What garlands!

As the record books show, it was not a damp race, and McGuinness did not have to settle for sixth or seventh. He led from start to finish. On lap two, slowing for the pit stop, he set a new lap record for the Superbike TT: 128.279mph. The HM Plant pit crew was just as impressive. Slick all week, they increased John's lead over Guy Martin by 6.5 seconds. By the end he was 26 seconds clear for a new race record of 1 hour 48m 11.17 seconds.

The shortage of garlands was not the only snag that day. When the three podium finishers were handed the customary champagne, John could not get the cork out. Guy and Hutchy were well into the ritual of spraying bubbly over all and sundry before the race winner finally coaxed the cork out of the bottle. This of course gave me something new to describe, which made for a bit of fun as well as livening up the commentary. One of the little challenges of the job is to describe those moments as the riders celebrate, the difficulty being that the routine is almost always identical and predictable. Corks pop, champagne is poured over rivals, brolly birds scuttle for cover, unsuspecting photographers get a soaking. Déjà vu seldom makes for lively radio but I tried to make it sound as if the whole thing was fresh and different. This time, thanks to the cork that wouldn't pop, it really was!

An innovation for 2007 was the installation of a speed trap on Sulby Straight. This was brilliant. The computer in front of me flicked up the speeds as the bikes thundered down the far side of the island. Hutchinson (Honda) 188.5, Martin (Honda) 185.9, Plater (Yamaha) 185.4, McGuinness (Honda) 182.9. There was so much information available that Norman Quayle and I had to make difficult decisions about which page of data we wanted. And the bikes were moving so fast it seemed no time at all before the data from, say, Ballaugh was being overtaken by the riders' arrival at Ramsey. No risk of déjà vu here.

The land of high expectations

The sidecar races in 2007 were among the most dramatic for many years. Nicky Crowe, partnered by Dan Sayle, was the pre-race favourite. In practice, Nicky was going well – he'd exceeded 114mph for the lap on both Tuesday and Thursday of Practice Week. When I chatted to him in the paddock he was confident of exceeding 115 under race conditions. With Molyneux suffering machine problems, as well as feeling his way back after his horrific crash in 2006, few argued with the notion that Crowe was the man to beat. But – and there's always a but on the Mountain Course – Nicky and Dan went off the start line in Race A like a rocket. At Glen Helen they were already five seconds up ... but they never made it to Ramsey. At Sulby the gearbox surrendered and the lads' race was over. Klaus Klaffenbock, who had controversially been given starting number four, retired at Ballacraine.

So it was all set up, then, for Molyneux? Not quite, because into the breach stepped Lancastrian John Holden. The Clitheroe man, third in

Race A for the last two years, led Molyneux by eight seconds after lap one, and was still ahead when they entered the third and final lap. I began checking my records for the last non-Manx winner of a Sidecar TT, but, as it turned out, Ian Bell's status in that respect was to remain unchallenged as the Moly magic returned. At Glen Helen for the last time he was in front. I remembered being given a hand-written press release just before the race, composed by Dave's wife Gaynor. It detailed many of the setbacks the team had experienced in preparing for this TT, and finished with the words: "Dave says no-one should expect too much." As Roy Moore handed back to me with Dave enjoying a three-second lead at the Hairpin I said: "Sorry Gaynor, but we're back in the land of high expectations again!" At the chequered flag, Moly and his chair-man Rick Long took it by over six seconds. After the trials and tribulations of 2006 it was the most emotional of victories. And for Rick it was a seventh TT win, having passengered Rob Fisher to six wins.

The second sidecar race had everything. It was one of the most crazy, unpredictable sporting events I've ever witnessed. The Open Golf Championship at Royal Birkdale in 1976 came close, when Sevvy Ballesteros first appeared on the scene and carved a brilliant but zany track in and out of the rough before narrowly losing to Johnny Miller. That, though, did not involve an all-time record, a hard luck story of gigantic proportions, a fairytale ending, and a dog. This one had the lot.

We were all set to go, and I was counting down the seconds to when Dave Molyneux on bike number one would set the race in motion. With a mere 12 seconds to go I spotted the 'race delayed' sign being waved at the front of the grid. I immediately relayed the delay, and all round the Grandstand there was a mass exhalation of disappointed breath, like the dismantling of a bouncy castle when rain cancels the kids' party.

The commentator's first job is to tell people what is happening. The second is to explain why. This time the first part was easy but the second was impossible until word came through from Race Control that a dog was loose on the course in the Glen Lough area. There would be a 15-minute delay. As it turned out, that delay was crucial because it enabled Molyneux to rectify an electrical fault. When Chief Minister Tony Brown returned to the rostrum to flag off the race, Molyneux and Long departed smoothly. But it was Crowe and Sayle who again tore into the lead. When they completed lap two at a new all-time sidecar record speed of 116.667, 19 minutes 24.24 seconds, they led by 38 seconds and were on their way to victory ... surely. But no. At Union Mills Crowe's engine blew and, for the second time in three days, it was race over. Molyneux, who had been no better than fourth at Glen Helen on lap one, took full advantage to win his 13th TT. John Holden took second and Steve Norbury third, but not without another piece of drama. Allan Schofield, the Wirral man who was also competing in the World Championship that year, inherited third place when Klaffenbock retired on lap three, and had his eyes on a first podium 11 years after his TT debut. But the black flag came out for Allan at the Bungalow (his machine was damaged after a coming-together with Gary Horspole at Ballaugh) and although he finished the race, the delay for the problem to be checked was enough for Steve Norbury and Simon Neary to sail past. Allan and his team-mate Peter Founds finished fifth, the same as in race one. In fact, the top seven places were identical in both sidecar events.

2007 was the year that a number of respected sidecar drivers bowed out. Among them were Dick Hawes and Dick Tapken, both racing for Brian Rostron's Dialled In Racing squad. When Hawes went to the line to start Race B it was his 67th TT race, another example of the magnetic pull of the Isle of Man. Not even a hip operation in January of 2007 could keep Dick away, but this, he told me, was definitely his farewell, and he would donate his machine to be used by newcomers in future. Dick had been a fantastic supporter of the races, combining the TT with racing commitments on the continent, where he won the Belgian Classic Championship in 2006, and took eighth pace on a G50 solo at Mettet, also in Belgium, less than a month before the 2007 TT. Dick Tapken, 'the Bloke from Stoke,' also called it a day on the island after finishing both races; a positive way to mark over half a century of races. In recounting the achievements of these two over the years, I almost talked my way into trouble by referring to 'the two Dicks ...' but, fortunately, I realised what was coming and managed to splutter my way out of trouble, like a classic two-stroke running wide at Governors.

Less fortunate was my old pal Dan Clark. After telling me the story of his dad's ashes in 2006, Dan had stopped in flames at Joey's in Race B. I was keen to find out what was the aftermath of that incident 12 months earlier. In Practice Week I tracked down Dan, lying flat on his back under his awning and looking as chilled as Ed Moses before the 400 metres hurdles. How was the urn? I had visions of the carefully-nurtured remains fluttering across Snaefell. "No problem," said Dan with a grin. "They're still intact." And sure enough, there was the urn, still bolted inside the fairing. But Dan and his passenger Nigel Mayers – returning to duty in the chair that year – had a nasty spill in practice and had to pull out of the races.

The three-wheeled brigade provided its customary clutch of good stories which had nothing to do with the results. That's the way it goes at the TT. Roy Hanks made his 75th start in Race B. Fiona Baker-Milligan teamed up with her dad Tony for the first time at the TT, while her sister Gail designed a logo for the fairing – two roses, symbolising Gail and mum Jennifer, to ensure that all four members of the family were represented on board. Eddy Wright returned to the island after an eight-year absence and raced against his son Doug – and on his debut, Doug and passenger Dips Chauhan took impressive 17th and 15th places, earning bronze replicas in both events. Ruth Laidlow failed to qualify for Race A, but made it into Race B to ensure that the Centenary TT at least had one female driver. And Japan, such a key nation in the history of the races, had a representative among the crews too – Masahito Watanabe and Yoshida Hideyuki entered their LCR Honda, managed by ex-TT competitor Masato Kumano, who, in 1976, had been the first Japanese sidecar driver to race here; they finished both races. My unofficial award for the best hairdo of the centenary went to Yorkshireman Brian Alflatt, whose remaining thatch was cut into a series of black and white tufts. The colour scheme, Brian explained, was inspired by the Shuttleworth Snap, the legendary bike ridden by George Formby in the film *No Limit*.

A 'mint' year

Centenary year was Honda year – the progeny of Soichiro Honda took five of the six victories. The one they missed was the Superstock, and that, once again, belonged to Suzuki and Bruce Anstey.

Postponed by 24 hours to allow Saturday's delayed programme to be accommodated on the Monday, the Superstock was flagged off by Pauline Jefferies, mother of ex-Suzuki ace DJ, and, appropriately, she saw the ensuing scrap dominated by Anstey. Bruce had taken part in a stunted photo, pretending to be asleep curled up on his bike, but this was wide-awake stuff as he led from start to finish, setting new lap records in the first two laps. The race was a tricky one for the pit crews – both Martin and Farquhar ran out of fuel, but the TAS team, unfamiliar that year in the black and white livery of its new sponsor Relentless, got it spot-on. Anstey won by 40 seconds from McGuinness, with Hutchinson third and Martin Finnegan taking the MV Agusta to a notable fourth place.

Wednesday at last saw us back on schedule when the Supersport race got away on the right day and at the right time; Murray Walker doing the honours as celebrity starter. It looked as if a double for Anstey was on the cards, but a lengthy pit stop cost him the lead, and a blistering effort over the final two laps by Ian Hutchinson earned him his first TT victory. Hutchy was fourth at the end of lap one but it's places at the chequered flag that count, and Ian's display on lap three proved decisive. Seven seconds down on McGuinness as they entered the pits after lap two, Ian was fractionally in front at Glen Helen on lap three, five seconds ahead at Ramsey, and on his way to his first TT win in a new race record time. After the tears and anger over that disqualification 12 months earlier, this was the perfect riposte. Little over a month later Ian would win his first British Supersports race when leading McGuinness over the line at Oulton Park.

Meanwhile, Guy Martin broke the 600cc lap record in a vain but heroic effort to improve on third place. Guy did 125.161mph on his final lap on the Hydrex Honda, finishing third. Two seconds, a third and a retirement made for a very good overall performance at the TT by a rider who became such good news for the event that he should have had a place on the Tourism Department executive committee. Now that would have livened up the meetings!

Guy is a bikeaholic. Show him a pair of wheels and he'll want to jump on board. Before the TT that year he entered the pre-TT Classic at Billown and won one of the races on a 750 Triumph Trident. At the Centenary Re-enactment he rode one of the vintage machines, and throughout the season he could be found bobbing between the Le Mans endurance race, road races and short circuits, 600s and superbikes, anything that provides a buzz. One evening at the TT I spotted him pedalling a pushbike down Douglas Prom, weaving in and out of the pedestrians like a man possessed. As an interviewee he was a reporter's dream. His enthusiasm fuelled a gift for communication and his words formed the sort of memorable quotes that journalists love. On his debut in 2004, he described Ian Lougher as travelling so fast he was "... sucking rabbits out of the hedge," a comment which lives on for its zest and originality. He is also a highly talented engineer whose love of motorcycling is intertwined with his ambition to tune the fastest, most reliable engines. Small wonder that visiting journalists quickly tracked down Guy to bring their despatches to life. And it's no surprise that he delivered. Despite being presented with champagne on a regular basis, Guy's favourite tipple is "... a good brew." And when he has a new buzz word, he uses it to distraction. In 2007, anything that was good was "mint." We heard a lot of "mint" in centenary year!

Competitors are drawn to the TT for all sorts of reasons. I chatted with Mark Parrett in his motorhome and discovered that his route lay via another motorsport event, the Manx Two-Day Trial. The trial was usually held a week before the Manx GP. Mark came over in 1987 to ride the trial as a passenger in the sidecar events and, after 11 years, became smitten by the preparations taking place around him for the Manx GP. He began racing in 1998, won the Manx in 2002, stepped up to the TT immediately, and got onto the podium in the Lightweight 400 in 2004.

"I love it," he said with a huge grin. "I couldn't race in 2005 because I did my collar bone at Scarborough, but I still came as a spectator. This year I'll be back for the Manx riding a G50. It's in the blood. My dad brought me when I was a boy to watch Mike Hailwood make his comeback in 1978, and now it's hard to imagine life without trips to the island."

Dad Jeff was there again, and although Mark had a frustrating time with three retirements, he did have the satisfaction of a creditable sixth place in the Superstock on his Yamaha R1, maintaining his record of never having a finish lower than 13th.

Race week in 2007 was idyllic. The weather was glorious, the island was packed and the atmosphere was wonderful. On one single evening on Douglas Promenade I watched beach motocross, tall ships out in the bay, daredevil stunts in front of the Villa, the Purple Helmets, and a breathtaking display by the Red Arrows. All free. On the Thursday, the organisers put on a mouth-watering event: a succession of mega names from motorcycling history appeared on a stage in front of the Grandstand to be interviewed and then have photos taken and sign autographs. The scenes at the rear of the stand where the ex-riders entered and departed were reminiscent of the stage door at a rock concert. And the queue for Giacomo Agostini's autograph literally blocked the thoroughfare in the tented village.

The paddock was spectacular, with all the main manufacturers represented in force. Bikes were readily available for spectators to inspect, merchandise was on sale, hospitality for corporate guests flourished. As a former Kawasaki owner it was great to see that Kawasaki had made a real effort this time, with a tasty display of classic machines on view. The contrast at the other end of the paddock was dramatic. While the big-budget teams blinged their way through TT 2007, Fabrice Miguet was raffling off his kit to help pay his bills. For £3 a ticket you could enter a draw to win his helmet. Second prize: a pair of racing gloves donated by his neighbours in the paddock, sidecar team Francois and Sylvie Leblond. But no-one was complaining. We were all just delighted to be there.

The first 130mph lap

And so to the Senior TT, the race that was the direct descendant of that original scrap on the roads around St John's in 1907. Instead of Frank Hulbert and Jack Marshall, the first two starters then, we had Michael Rutter and Adrian Archibald setting things in motion, and for Michael, a well-deserved eighth-place, finish having retired in his other two races. Adrian got home in fifth place, another welcome achievement after retirements in the Supersport and Superstock. But the day was all about the man who left the grid with plate number three, John McGuinness.

Let me fast-forward a couple of days to the Sunday evening. On the ferry to Heysham I was tapped on the shoulder and a voice said, "You were getting a bit carried away over that 130 business, weren't you?" It was John himself, big grin on face. He was right, of course. He'd heard the recording of the moment when he came into the pits at the end of lap two and I'd informed the world of that orbit-breaking moment. Would the 130mph lap be done this year? I'd been speculating as the HM Plant Honda braked into the stop box. And then, as the computer line in front of me updated: "It *has* been done! It HAS been done!!" Listening again later, I could tell that the engineers were frantically winding the volume down because my voice was busting the decibels at the top end! 130.354mph was the new record, and McGuinness, aided by two more superb pit stops by his crew, wheelied past the chequered flag in a new race record time. A hundred years after Charlie Collier won it on a Matchless, McGuinness was equal to Collier in one respect: matchless. This was win number 13, Honda's 135th, and a clean sweep of the podium for Honda, with Guy Martin second and Ian Hutchinson third.

Steve Linsdell was one of many riders who didn't reach the finish. Steve was riding a 500cc Paton twin, specially entered for the centenary. The Paton, produced by the Italian manufacturer as the spare bike for its 2001 Grand Prix campaign, had never been raced until 2007 on the Isle of Man. The team had developed a special logo combining the Paton name and the TT initials. The team's involvement spoke volumes for the affection in which the TT is held, even by people who are not regulars on the road racing scene, like company boss Roberto Patoni who was there in person. Steve was forced to retire the bike at Bishopscourt on lap four, but the Paton provided a lovely dash of the unorthodox at an event inevitably dominated by Japanese machinery.

My verdict on the Centenary TT is that it didn't live up to expectations – it surpassed them, and that's saying a lot. The hype was extraordinary, and built up over a two to three year period. It seemed an impossible task for the Government, the Department of Tourism and Leisure, the Manx Motorcycle Club and all the other authorities to deliver something which would please everyone – but they did it.

There were a lot of grumbles about the Steam Packet Company, whose schedules were stretched beyond breaking point – my return crossing was changed three times, and I heard a lot of similar stories from very frustrated travellers. But time smooths over the ruts and allows the memory to focus on the good moments. Everyone who was on the island in June 2007 will have plenty of those. One of them for me was describing Carl Fogarty lead off the *MCN* centenary parade after the Senior. Foggy was in his pomp when I began covering the TT for BBC TV, and as a Lancashire-based sportsman he was one of the personalities I'd interviewed for *North West Tonight* on many occasions. Carl Fogarty riding again at the TT – that was something special. Seeing John Surtees in action was another great thrill. The sportsmen and women who are stars when we are kids have a special place in the hearts of all sports followers, and Surtees filled that spot for me, as an imperious motorbike racer in my early years and then as a four-wheeled winner in my early teens. I saw – and heard – him drive a very raucous F1 Honda car at Oulton Park in the days when the Gold Cup attracted the top motor racing names to Cheshire every September.

So many teams and individuals made extra efforts because 2007 was centenary year. Hans-Peter Bolliger, better known for his Bolliger Kawasaki World Endurance team, went to huge trouble and expense to bring two bikes and full support to the island. Hans-Peter and his colleague Stefan Kuehn of SK Support got a raw deal when Michael Weynand crashed in practice and ruled himself out of the races completely, but Gary Carswell, their other rider, scored 16th and 13th places in the two superbike races, and earned bronze replicas in both. For a short time in 2007, Gary was the fastest Manxman ever, but Conor Cummins overtook him in the Senior – Conor, another rider who achieved great things that year with a fifth, two sixths and an eighth, all at the age of 21. The centenary was a good year for him, as it was for Steve Plater, Jimmy Moore, Gary Johnson, Keith Amor, Ian Armstrong, James McBride and Ian Pattinson.

We had two final visitors to the commentary box – German rider Thomas Schoenfelder and his new bride Simone. Twelve months earlier Thomas proposed to Simone live on Radio TT. Now they were celebrating their wedding which had taken place the previous day at Douglas Registry Office. Seeing Thomas and Simone full of smiles was a good way to bid farewell to the Centenary TT, and one more reminder that this is one sporting event where you don't have to win to feel good about yourself. There was one final celebration: Anthony Pugh presented Eunice with a framed photograph to mark her 25 years as producer of these very testing broadcasts, a nice touch and the recognition was well deserved.

The best moment for me, of course, was being the commentator who described the first 130mph lap on the hundredth birthday of the world's most spectacular motorsport event.

2008 – Manna from heaven for a live broadcaster

Too much bad news

The build-up to the first TT of the second centenary was awful. In March the coroner's report into the deaths at the 26th Milestone was released, containing strong criticism of many of those involved in running the event. By this time the Manx Motorcycle Club had already resigned as organiser of the TT. Whether this was because it foresaw the likely outcome of the inquest was unclear, but it would have been difficult for individuals like Neil Hanson to carry on after the coroner, Michael Moyle, had his say. I felt very sorry for Neil, a courteous and decent man who would never do anything which was likely to increase the inevitable risks to riders. The fact remained, though, that Moyle uncovered evidence of confusion regarding the designation, marking and supervising of prohibited areas, and this had been a major factor in the deaths of the two unfortunate spectators. For 2008, a number of familiar faces would be absent from the administration. Roger Hurst, the chief marshal, was another casualty as a wind of change swept through the corridors of power. And the running of the TT was now in the hands of the Auto Cycle Union's subsidiary, ACU Events Ltd.

At the start of May came the terrible news that Martin Finnegan had been killed in a racing accident at Tandragee in Northern Ireland. It was devastating. Martin was such a talented rider as well as being a charismatic individual who had brought so much pleasure to the TT. Whether playing Jenga in the pub or sliding round Ramsey Hairpin like a kid on a tea-tray he did everything to the maximum and carried everyone else along with him. I remembered his aerobatics over the bridge at Ballaugh, and a sensational still photograph of Martin at the bottom of Barregarrow, bike bottoming out, face a mask of concentration. It was hard to accept that he wouldn't have the chance to build on his one podium finish, third, on the Vitrans Ten Kate Honda in the 2006 Superbike TT.

Then, just as we were preparing to leave the house in Liverpool to fly to Northern Ireland for the NW 200 I was told that Robert Dunlop had lost his life in a crash in practice the previous evening. His bike had apparently seized, and, as he came off, he was struck by the following rider Darren Burns, who himself suffered fractures. We arrived in Belfast to find no other story on the front pages, while, south of the border, RTE's afternoon radio phone-in discussed no other topic. Robert, like his brother Joey, was a giant of road racing, with five TT wins under his belt, a tally which would surely have been many more but for a serious accident at Ballaugh in 1994. In 2008 he was due to return to the TT, having entered both the 125 and 250 races at Billown. Robert's return was eagerly anticipated, but it was not to be.

It was yet another cruel blow and these are times when you really wonder why you bother with a sport which can hurt people so much. But motorcycle racing has a hold which cannot be broken, and the Dunlop family would prove that yet again.

This was my first visit to the NW 200, and we arrived on the Causeway Coast in time to witness one of the most sensational displays of courage in the sports arena that I have ever come across. Less than 48 hours after the death of his dad, and only the day before the funeral, Michael Dunlop went out and won the 250cc race. It was incredible.

Both Michael, then 20, and his elder brother William were entered to ride, but both indicated they would withdraw after the accident. They changed their minds, only for William's bike to break down before the start. Michael then took part in an amazing battle with Christian Elkin and John McGuinness before snatching the lead on the last lap and holding on to win the most emotional of victories. If anyone ever doubted what a sporting victory can mean to a family, this raised the bar to a new level. For the TT, however, Michael and William were both adamant that there would be no Dunlop on the start list this time.

The teams, media, officials and spectators who headed for the island in the middle of the Irish Sea at the end of May did so in an uncertain state of mind, unsure of what to expect. One thing I could definitely expect as the commentator was the huge amount of work that is always required when preparing for a job like this. Much of that involves research which is never actually used, but you do it anyway (partly from the professionalism of the job, but also because there is some nagging compulsion which forces you onwards even when you are pretty sure that you are going down a cul-de-sac).

Two days into my stay on the island for TT 2008 I was sitting in my room, pondering a note which I'd made the previous year about Geoff

Duke. It referred to Geoff's involvement in the Manx Grand Prix of 1948 which was, of course, 60 years before, a milestone worth mentioning. Checking the exact details of Geoff's contribution in 1948 then took far, far longer than any airtime which would be filled by a quick mention. Out came my copy of *The History of the Manx Grand Prix* by Bill Snelling and Peter Kneale. Then Stuart Barker's excellent *100 Years of the Isle of Man Tourist Trophy*. That prompted a check of the official online TT database. In no time my room was a becoming the familiar mess of books, paper, notes and magazines. It felt good to be back!

But how many more people were back? Out on Douglas Promenade it was quiet. Okay, it's always quiet at the very start of Practice Week. And no-one could possibly expect a repeat of the crowds and the buzz that came in for the centenary. But I found it hard to agree with the official forecasts that the number of visitors to TT 2008 would exceed those of 2006. The evidence of my own eyes didn't back that up, and as the fortnight progressed my view didn't change. Even in Race Week you could park a four-wheeled vehicle on the prom without too much difficulty. Driving around the island I saw nothing like the usual squadrons of bikers out on the roads. The usual hotspots for parked bikes were busy, but not as busy as usual – in my personal, non-statistical opinion.

I was told that more visitors were staying out of Douglas in 2008 because there were fewer hotel rooms in the capital. That could certainly have been true. The Castle Mona cut a forlorn, mothballed figure, and anyone who normally stayed there would definitely have had to find pastures new. But the feeling persisted that this was not the very well-attended TT that the authorities had hoped for. Several weeks later, official figures from the Steam Packet confirmed that passenger numbers were down 19 per cent on 2007 – and seven per cent on 2006!

In the paddock, this was mirrored to a degree by the absence of a number of teams who had dug deep to participate in the centenary. No Bolliger Kawasaki team, for example. A greater blow was the decision of the Honda works setup to stay away this time. The HM Plant supported team had competed at the NW 200 but the island was not on its agenda this year. Instead, John McGuinness was riding for a team created by the fusion of Padgett's, the well-known motorcycle dealership from Yorkshire, and Manx Gas, although many of the personnel behind him were the familiar crew. John's team-mate from 12 months earlier, Ian Hutchinson, was now with Alistair Flanagan's AIM Yamaha team.

In a way, this made 2008 an even more exciting prospect, with a number of riders from different teams all having a genuine chance: McGuinness would be challenged by Guy Martin in Hydrex Honda Bike Animal colours, Bruce Anstey and Cameron Donald in the Relentless

Suzuki by TAS squad, and Hutchinson and Steve Plater for AIM Yamaha. The appearance of Conor Cummins with plate number two added an intriguing local element to the contest, although it would be Ryan Farquhar who emerged as the joker in the pack.

My first target, though, did not concern the upcoming duels on the Mountain Course. It was to get up to speed with the situation at Billown.

Battered but not beaten

The first TT of the second century was historic in that it included two races at Billown, the 4.25 mile course in the south of the island. After much debate, 125cc and 250cc machines would once again race for TT trophies, making Billown the fourth course to stage TT racing, and the first apart from the Mountain Course since the Clypse Course was used in the 1950s. The races, plus a 600cc/1000cc support race, would be staged the day after the Senior, on the traditional day of the Steam Packet Races, with the Steam Packet company still involved as sponsor.

When the announcement was made I discussed the situation with Tim Glover. I wanted to be involved but I had no wish to supplant Maurice as the resident commentator on the start/finish line. My suggestion was that Maurice should do his usual excellent job and I would do the introductions, ceremonies, and interview the bigwigs. The plan was quickly abandoned when Maurice revealed that, before the new TT races had been announced, he had taken up an offer to attend the US Open, which entailed leaving the island the day of the Billown races. "That means it's you in the commentary box," said Tim. Unpleasant memories of 2005 came flooding back. I couldn't afford any cock-ups this time, with TT races at stake. So the Monday of Practice Week, when the Blackford's Pre-TT Classic meeting took place at Billown, found me standing behind Maurice watching his every move with forensic attention to detail!

Newcomers to any commentating situation find that one of the challenges is getting used to the routine of that event. Once you've achieved that, the whole thing becomes more straightforward. You know what will happen next without thinking. But at first, it can be mind-blowingly complex, and, again, careful preparation is in order.

An example of what I mean is the sign that an official shows to the riders on the grid at Billown. Once they've assembled, a sign is hoisted on a long pole and shown to the competitors. Sitting right behind, the radio commentator can see the words: 'Watch Lights.' The unsuspecting newcomer would be justified in thinking that the riders are seeing the same message. Then the sign is swivelled 180 degrees and the commentator now sees: 'Engage Gear.' This, of course, is what the riders saw just before. So clocking that and understanding it is a key part of the job. Failure to do so would guarantee that the commentary would get off to a dismal start.

I made a point of going out of the box and along the grass to see exactly what the riders saw. I watched as the red lights, mounted on the corner of the control building, which included the commentary box, went out to signal the start of the race. I made a note of many other details, such as the way Maurice was advised of non-starters, grid positions, final results, lap records, and so on. Every now and again Control would ring down with news of retirements. That meant I would need someone to answer the phone – not a task I could manage while live on air. That would be Tim Glover's role. Maurice's wife, Marilyn, did that job normally, as well as looking out for approaching riders and channelling information back and forth: a vital role which should not be under-estimated.

It was a good day's racing, which produced some unexpected drama when Guy Martin came off his bike just as victory was his for the taking. The battery worked loose and lodged against the wheel, causing the bike to lock up and spit him off. It was a freakish accident but, sadly, proved to be a foretaste of Guy's entire TT that year. It was also a good day's preparation for me, and I was looking forward to describing the scene when we reassembled on the Castletown Bypass to watch TT racing in the south of the island.

Back behind the TT Grandstand I caught up with Dan Clark. His TT the previous year had ended in a spectacular smash in practice. I didn't know if he would be here this time but soon came across him, sitting under the awning of sidecar driver Michael Lines, dispensing advice from between a pair of crutches.

Clearly his injuries from last year were far from healed. "I got out of hospital on my 60th birthday, and I've been back in 36 times since January," he declared, with an attention to statistics that Norman Quayle would have admired. He listed the damage, which included a broken left leg, two fractured ribs, and numerous other ailments. He produced a series of still photos of the crash which were not exactly the sort of material the Department of Tourism would use. "And I've had to retire from my job." Remembering that he worked as a health and safety advisor for his local authority, this might have come as some form of reassurance to the public!

But here he was, back at the TT, living proof that the magnetism of the event simply can't be neutralised by anything as trivial as a life-threatening prang. Worryingly, Dan was talking about a comeback. "I'm not retiring on a crash," he asserted. "I've still got one race left in me." His friends did not seem keen on this idea.

Dan was here to support Michael Lines who was competing at the TT for the first time. This was an interesting reversal of the usual process. It's not unusual for a rider to go on to run a team or even sponsor one, but not so the other way round. Michael had been Dan's sponsor but now he was out there himself. He had been coming to the TT for some 20 years, and had raced sidecars in England where he won the North Gloucester championship in 2007 and drove his 600cc machine to second place in the Open class. He had teamed up with Mike Aylott, who was also making his TT debut. Mike was grinning from ear to ear at the prospect – and gave an insight into the true camaraderie of this event.

"I've had a lot of help from people," he told me. "Dave Wallis, Mark Cox, Patrick Farrance. Patrick has given me his notes for the whole circuit. But of course, everyone is different. Different size, weight, machine. You can get all the help going but you still have to work it out for yourself."

He'd already endured one problem. On an early practice lap the tube had come out of the drinks bottle tucked inside his leathers. "The juice squirted all over me and I was covered in liquid all the way round."

The sidecar entrants were in great shape. The bikes and crews all looked smart, and created a wonderful spectacle lining up for practice laps. The races were a fascinating prospect, with Manx aces Dave Molyneux and Nick Crowe fit and raring to go, and England's John Holden packing extra punch thanks to a deal with Hector Neill's Relentless by TAS team. "TAS have supplied an engine, and I reckon I've got an extra 20bhp this year. I've got a new LCR chassis, and we're leading the British Championship, so things are going well."

I asked Hector about the deal. "I wanted to give the boys some help, and, to be honest, I thought Relentless would come up with some backing," he replied. "In the end they didn't, so I've sorted them out with something myself." The TAS support, which included full livery on the fairing and team kit for John and his passenger Andy Winkle, made a great impression. At the same time Honda was supplying Nicky Crowe's engines, and the sidecar grid was really well tooled up. A number of crews had switched to Suzuki engines this year, including Dave Molyneux, and it was also noticeable how many LCR machines were out there. It was only four years since Louis Christian had supplied just two drivers with his new chassis; now there were 14.

Not everyone thought the LCR was wonderful. Bill Currie, still competitive at the age of 65, had carried out a number of modifications to his. But the rest seemed very content, including Nicky Crowe.

Nicky's whole operation seemed to have moved up a gear. His PR was eye-catching, with the slogan 'as the Crowe flies' much in evidence. His pitch in the paddock now included a smart hospitality area where visitors arrived to find a piece of topiary cut in the shape of a crow planted at the entrance! "Last year was such a disappointment, and also a huge blow financially," he told me. "Now we are ready to go again, and we have support from Honda, which gives us much more flexibility in terms of replacing engines." His two retirements in 2007 had cost him heavily in the wallet, and he'd had to contend with a badly broken leg (and just as much embarrassment) when falling off a moped on holiday, plus a broken collar bone early in the season. But he looked remarkably calm as well as very determined. The sidecar races would be worth watching.

The TT paddock always offers interesting hairstyles, including the facial variety. My unofficial award for the best beard of 2008 went to Irishman Pete Farrelly, for the near waist-length creature swarming out of his chin. How did he cope with all that under his helmet? "I plait it and throw it over my shoulder," he said with a beam. And what was behind the name of his entrant, Reptile Racing? "I'm a tiler."

Pete and his passenger Jason Miller picked up two bronze replicas for their efforts, and gave us a good laugh as well.

The flying Crowe and leathers round the ankles

I was not the only one who was looking forward to the sidecar races with even more expectation than usual. Dave Molyneux versus Nicky Crowe promised to be a gripping duel, spiced up by the added punch coming from John Holden. We also had Tim Reeves making his IOM debut, the first reigning World Sidecar Champion to contest the TT in almost 30 years.

The first of the three-wheeled races gave us a typical moment of TT drama. Moly was off at number one, bang on schedule at 3pm on the opening Saturday, but as he moved off the line and passed my vantage point it was obvious the bike was not getting up to speed. I commented on the fact, but at least Moly was racing, and my eyeline switched to the lap record holder, Nicky, who was next to go. At that moment I heard Chris Kinley's voice howling in my headphones, to the effect that Molyneux was pulling off the track. He was out of my line of vision so I immediately handed down to Chris who reported the news that Moly and Dan Sayle, back in the chair this year, had stopped. Their race was over already with what turned out to be a problem with the clutch. This left the race open for Nicky – or did it? At Glen Helen it was Holden who led, and it was still the Lancashire driver with passenger Andy Winkle who were in front at the halfway stage. Nicky and Mark Cox were never far behind, though, and, at Ramsey on lap two, Roy Moore reported that they had taken the lead by four seconds.

That was the decisive moment, and Crowe and Cox built a steady lead through to the chequered flag, waved this year by Paul Kermode, successor to Andy Fern.

The race was notable for a string of high profile retirements, not just Moly: Klaus Klaffenbock went out on lap one, while Steve Norbury retired on lap two when lying third, and Simon Neary bowed out on the last lap, also when third. John Holden came through to secure the runners-up spot, and the retirements paved the way for Tim Reeves to snatch an amazing and very creditable third on his TT debut. He was the first newcomer to reach the podium since Jock Taylor in 1978, and he was delighted to prove the doubters wrong. "We've pissed on their cornflakes," was the colourful way he described his elation live on air with Chris.

Before the second sidecar race got under way on the Wednesday I was musing about the athletics careers of Sebastian Coe and Steve Ovett. It struck me that we had a very similar situation, albeit for different reasons. In the mid-eighties, Coe and Ovett were the two best middle distance runners in the world. Yet the two Brits never seemed to race each other. Not wanting to lose face by losing, they would turn up in the big events in different races – sometimes running in dubious races like the 600 metres, which had no genuine status, in order to bring in the punters but avoid the risk of either being beaten. What we all wanted on the Isle of Man in 2008 was a head-to-head duel between the two Manx superstars, Dave Molyneux and Nicky Crowe. Fate, though, was always conspiring against it. They weren't dodging each other the way Coe and Ovett did, but if one had a good race the other broke down or crashed out. That Wednesday in 2008 was the day it all changed.

It was a sunny but windy day. Simon Last-Sutton of sponsor Sure Mobile flagged them away, and Moly got off to a good start this time. So did Nicky, though, and, at Glen Helen he was ahead by two seconds. At Ramsey it was five seconds. When the machines scorched past us at the Grandstand at the end of lap one Crowe and Cox had Molyneux and Sayle in their sights, only two seconds behind on the road, eight seconds up on corrected time. It was an epic duel, filmed by the expert cameras of the Greenlight production company from positions around the track and aloft in the helicopter. Throughout laps two and three the two outfits raced cheek by jowl. It was Crowe who led across the line to win by 10.5 seconds, completing the double for the second time in his career, his sixth TT win, no longer the apprentice but very much the sorcerer, a true star of the Mountain Course who, at last, had beaten the old maestro Molyneux in face-to-face combat.

As for the solo racing in 2008, the start was a complete shambles. It was also an episode which underlined the value of experience which, thankfully, I now had a fair amount of. If this had been my first year in the box I'm not sure if I would have had a clue what was going on. Or, to be accurate, what was not going on.

The starting procedure at the TT is a well-established routine. Signals are given at regular intervals by klaxon and by the display of boards telling the riders how long remains to the start. Riders line up in race order on Glencrutchery Road, and are ushered to the start line in good time. This year there was an innovation, in that a temporary starting gate was built – a rectangular archway under which the rider would be poised, ready to explode into action. This structure brought an added touch of drama to the start, especially for TV and DVD consumers who would see something like the scene at certain rugby league games where the teams emerge from an archway with smoke billowing and fireworks cracking. Except the smoke and fireworks here came from the bikes themselves. I wasn't sure this was much of an advantage for some of the spectators on the far side of the road whose view of the bikes racing off towards Bray Hill might be completely blocked, but still, it was an interesting development.

The seconds ticked down to the 12 noon start of the Superbike TT, and it was clear that bike number one, belonging to Guy Martin, was not there. My eyes were flicking between the guest starter, Lino Dainese, of the company that makes the leathers and was sponsoring the race, and the starting arch. Ten seconds to go and still no bike. At noon the starter's flag dropped and nothing happened. Suddenly Guy appeared and the Hydrex Honda roared off, but already the flag was dropping for the second starter, Conor Cummins. Conor appeared from behind the archway and shot off. Third off was John McGuinness who just about made his allotted slot but didn't have the chance to bring the bike to a standstill; it was virtually a rolling start. This was farcical. The riders were having no chance to compose themselves and focus their thoughts before the start of this uniquely tricky race. Fortunately, things settled down after that and the remaining riders got away in good order. It turned out that Guy Martin had been in the toilet!

At the same time there appeared to have been a complete lack of urgency and awareness among everyone else that the start of the race was upon us. I suppose everyone was waiting for the first rider in the queue to make the move towards the line, but if he was in the portaloo with his leathers round his ankles ...

From the commentator's point of view this sort of incident is both good and bad news. Good news because it's something unexpected, and therefore of interest to the audience. All around the course, and indeed around the world of the internet, I could imagine people following the description of events with complete incredulity. The bad news is that you, the person with the mic, haven't a clue what's going on, or why, or what will happen next. All you can do is describe the scene in front of you and react as anyone would. If you don't know the reasons for what you are seeing, say so. If you are baffled, make that clear. If you have theories as to what might be amiss, by all means voice them, but avoid jumping to conclusions. This sort of unscheduled 'entertainment' is embarrassing for the organisers but manna from heaven for a live broadcaster.

Which brings me back to the value of experience. If this had taken place in 2004, my first year, I would have been completely thrown. No doubt about it. I wouldn't have been up to speed on the usual routine so I couldn't have spoken with authority about the extent to which this was out of the ordinary. Happily, the commentary got off to a decent start even if the race didn't.

The TT started the way it would go on for Guy Martin. It just wasn't his year. He shattered the Superbike TT lap record on lap one, and improved it again on lap two, only to retire at Sulby Village on lap four when leading. Guy was also forced into premature exits in both the first Supersport race and the Senior, when he made his return to the Grandstand in the back of a furniture van. His only podium was third place in the Superstock, a big disappointment after twice taking the runners-up spot 12 months earlier.

Guy was not the only high profile retiree from that opening race. Ian Hutchinson and Conor Cummins also bowed out, and McGuinness called it a day on lap two after pulling in at Glen Helen where he finally got to meet Maurice Mawdsley face-to-face. Not the circumstances either of them would have liked, but John's demeanour when he gave his unscheduled interview to Maurice showed how amazingly level-headed he is – one minute grappling with a heavy race bike at lunatic speeds, the next chatting as if he'd just strolled into the pub. Although I wouldn't expect any of the three riders to agree, it was perhaps just as well that neither John, Conor nor Guy finished the race, because the repercussions of those delayed starts would hardly bear thinking about.

Men from down under

The winner of the Superbike TT was the man who started at plate number six, Cameron Donald. Cameron was riding in only his third TT after missing 2007 through injury. He went into this opening race as if he'd never been away, holding a steady second place for the first three laps and moving into the lead when Martin retired at Sulby on lap four. He came into the pits at the end of the lap almost side-by-side with Anstey who had started ten seconds ahead of him, the two TAS team-mates over a minute ahead of Adrian Archibald. The pit stops failed to alter the time difference and spectators were treated to the spectacle of the two Suzukis dicing round the last two laps, Cameron covering every attempt by Bruce to break away, before the Aussie led the Kiwi over the line in a new race record of 1 hour 47 minutes 5.89 seconds. It was a terrific performance by Cameron and a superb achievement by the Relentless by TAS team.

Archibald clinched third to make it an all-Suzuki podium, and it was great to see Adrian up there again after three difficult years. Adrian was now running his own AMA setup, but had assistance from TAS which only added to the celebrations. Gary Johnson was an excellent fourth.

As Cameron closed in on victory it occurred to me that his family at home – in Warrandyte just outside Melbourne – would be following his progress via Manx Radio TT's internet service. That is one of the wonderful developments of the 21st century: enabling TT fans to follow the races every step of the way, no matter where they are in the world.

That thought was confirmed for me at the prize presentation in the Villa Marina 48 hours later. "My brother recorded the closing stages of the race commentary, and when I called home he played it back to me down the phone," Cameron told me. "It made the hairs stand up on the back of my neck." And he went on to thank me for providing the words for his folks to follow.

Those sentiments from Cameron meant a lot. And it was so thoughtful of him to bother. By this time he was a double TT winner, having also collected the trophy for the Superstock race on the Monday morning. This time he'd snatched the lead from McGuinness in the first few miles of lap two, a lead the TAS team improved at the pit stop to bring Cameron home with 15 seconds in hand. Anstey retired after lap one, feeling unwell, McGuinness took second and Guy Martin third.

2008 saw the return of a second race for the 600s. It was a good move – the race programme had been somewhat lacking for the previous couple of years, the gap filled by an extra parade for centenary year. So, with little time to recover, Cameron and the rest were out on Glencrutchery Road in the afternoon.

It turned out to be the most controversial race of the TT that year. Anstey led from start to finish, 21 seconds ahead of Steve Plater's Yamaha at the chequered flag. But after we had gone off air came the news that Bruce's bike had failed the post-race checks because the exhaust camshafts didn't meet specifications. Plater was elevated to top spot, with McGuinness now second and Keith Amor third. For Plater and Amor, these were really special achievements. For each of them it was only their second year at the TT. Plater, somewhat ahead of schedule, confirmed his outstanding ability as a motorcycle racer.

On the Wednesday, with races still departing on schedule, there could only be one winner. John Reynolds, the three-times British Superbike Champion and a former TT rider himself in 1989, flagged them away. Ian Hutchinson led at the end of lap one, but Bruce was right on his case and led all the way from Glen Helen on lap two. Ryan

Farquhar took third place, his first podium since winning the 600 race in 2005.

The Manx Radio TT team was functioning well, too. Our only change was the departure of Tony Heron from his role as one of the engineers in the main box at the Grandstand. Tony had moved on to a new job, which meant the box was notably quieter when his countryman Anstey was in the lead! Bob Allison moved from Ramsey to the Grandstand, and Mike Reynolds took over engineering responsibility at the Hairpin. There was one unscheduled addition to the commentary team. Midway through the second Supersport race I felt my bum being fondled, and it didn't feel like my wife doing the fondling. I was in full flow at the time and glanced round to see the outright lap record holder grinning at me. John McGuinness had made his way up after retiring in the pits. "Right mate," I thought, "I'll get you for that," and thrust the microphone into his hand. "Get on with it!"

"Adrian Archibald there," he began. "Sun glinting on the fairing ..."

If anyone was crazy enough to propose a job swap, John would have no difficulty with his part of the deal.

It had been a very good week's racing. Good weather, lively racing, and a dash of controversy. And it was all leading up to a grand finale.

The Isle of Sam

The paddock at the TT is like a rain forest – teeming with life, as naturalists like David Attenborough would say. It isn't just a place where oily mechanics wrestle with gearboxes. At any given time there are all manner of activities going on – families having parties, deals being done, goods being sold, prayers being said. Halfway through Race Week I came across an artist working away under an awning. He had a part-finished portrait of Phil Read on his easel. His name was Bert Wouters, from Belgium, a relative by marriage of Bert Vloemans, Alan Warner's sidecar passenger. Bert Wouters didn't speak much English, but thanks to his niece Inge I worked out that he had been coming to the TT for several years, and took commissions which he'd work on over the winter and deliver the following year.

Who are his favourite riders? "Agostini, Hailwood and Guy Martin," came the reply, which seemed a very fair line-up.

The paddock was also the setting for one of the more poignant moments. I discovered that Martin Finnegan had wanted one of the special Arai Centenary helmets the previous year but never got round to picking one up. He had arranged to collect one from Adrian Crossan's mobile display this year. The helmet was still in Adrian's truck, and was being raffled off at £5 a ticket to raise money for Martin's family. I heard about this while having coffee in Ramsey one morning when we got talking to a couple who were sitting nearby. They introduced themselves as Kevin Evans and Josie Truelove, from the Midlands. During our chat they mentioned the story about Martin and the helmet. I duly called in at the Crossan emporium, which is always one of the most eye-catching displays, situated at the end of the Grandstand, and the story checked out. I was able to give it a mention over the air.

Around the same time Dorothy and I kept bumping into another couple with their two kids. It was spooky. Everywhere we went, this family seemed to be there too, and we'd exchange a few words – the Grandstand, Ramsey, Niarbyl, and finally Port Erin. This time we spoke in greater detail and established that they were Julie and Ian from Leicestershire, staunch TT supporters. They were due to be married the following August. Where? At the Manx Grand Prix of course!

Talk about the place being in your blood. And thus it was for Michael Dunlop, who had turned up halfway through Practice Week with his R6 in the van, and promptly picked up James McBride's ride with the Phase One team. James had come a cropper on the first Monday, crashing at Gorse Lea, just before Ballacraine. Two days later I bumped into his partner Dorothy and little girl Molly, sorting bits and pieces in the truck. James had numerous fractures but was pulling through. Michael was having an astounding TT: 14th in the superbike race, tenth and eighth in the two Supersports. Not for the first time I was reminded that this event is not just about the podium finishers. It's also about the many human dramas of one kind or another that seem to flourish at the TT.

The morning of the Senior TT was warm and sunny. The pre-race formalities had an extra zing. Samantha Barks, a Laxey girl who had been a sensation in the BBC TV series *I'd Do Anything*, was back on the island having been voted out after reaching the last three. Her image had been all over the island for weeks, with viewers from the 'Isle of Sam' running up hefty phone bills voting. Sam had accepted an invitation to sing the Manx National Anthem which she did, expertly. For once, John McGuinness found himself upstaged in the quest for autographs. The VIP party also included Mark Cavendish, the cycling star, one of that incomprehensible breed who enjoy riding very long distances without the assistance of an engine.

The Senior was due off at noon which gave the right amount of time for a parade of Ducati machinery, to mark 50 years of racing by the Bologna factory and 30 years since Mike Hailwood made his celebrated comeback on one of the Italian machines.

Just how lasting Hailwood's legacy has been was rammed home that week. So many people trace their TT allegiance back to that summer of 1978. Among them was George Spence who was marking his own tenth anniversary as a competitor. "I first came in 1978 to watch Mike

Hailwood and that got me hooked," he told me in the paddock. James Whitham was another one. James, a much respected racer himself, of course, now a TV commentator, wrote an evocative piece in the magazine *Island Racer*, recalling how he was brought by his dad in 1978, dismissed Hailwood as an over-the-hill has-been, but went home to Yorkshire with stars in his eyes, converted.

Ducati played its part by exhibiting a display of its finest machines in the newly refurbished pavilion in Noble's Park, Mike's No 12 bike having pride of place. His son David rode a replica in the parade. This time there was only one Ducati on the grid for the Senior. Once again it would be a shoot-out between the Japanese manufacturers.

I was well aware that Honda had so far failed to win any of the solo races. Quite a contrast from 2007, and I checked back as far as 1981 before finding a year when it hadn't won a solo race at the TT. Would it pay the ultimate price for its decision not to commit fully this time? Was the emergence of Cameron Donald and Steve Plater a sign that the changing of the guard was upon us? Was it heck!

The record books show that John McGuinness and Honda did it again, but they don't tell the full story. This was a sensational race, gripping from start to finish with the lead changing hands no fewer than eight times as McGuinness, Donald and Anstey went for it with no holds barred. McGuinness was fastest as far as Ramsey, but Anstey was superb over the mountain and led when they passed my position in the Grandstand – but by less than half a second, with Cameron 0.47 seconds further back. Entering the pits after lap two, John was only 1.7 seconds down, but there was drama as Bruce climbed off the bike, beaten by clutch trouble. On lap three it was McGuinness in front at Glen Helen, Donald at Ramsey, and McGuinness again at the Grandstand. The second pit stop saw Cameron leap ahead, and, embarking on the sixth and last lap it looked like he was on for a hat-trick of wins – 4.7 seconds ahead of the Honda. Meanwhile, Martin had gone out at Quarterbridge on lap three, and Archibald was out at Ballacraine.

At Glen Helen Maurice Mawdsley was waiting for Donald to confirm his lead, but sensationally it was McGuinness who led once more. By the time they reached the Hairpin John had a comfortable lead, with the Suzuki struggling with an oil leak. On the day we celebrated Mike Hailwood, winner of 14 TTs, we also saluted a true hero of the modern era, as McGuinness wrapped up his own 14th win with over 50 seconds in hand.

It was a superb sporting event, with Cameron nursing the Suzuki home for second place, Hutchy taking the Yamaha into third, and Ryan Farquhar earning fourth for Kawasaki – the top four places, unusually, occupied by four different marques. Ryan had a great TT. Having split with McAdoo a week before practice started he did sensationally well to reel off sixth, fourth, fourth, third and fourth, especially as he was riding Kenny Harker's superstock ZX10 in the two big-bike races. Gary Johnson enhanced his reputation with four top-six finishes, Michael Dunlop took tenth in the Senior, and it was a good TT also for Carl Rennie, Dan Stewart, Ian Pattinson, Mark Parrett, Ian Mackman, and two fast newcomers from England, James Hillier and Jamie Robinson. Many riders receive barely a mention throughout the TT, but still go home with a terrific feeling of achievement. Among them this time was Rob Barber, 27 years of age from Bury, who wrapped up his 2008 campaign by piloting Dave Cottrill's Suzuki to 20th place in the Senior, Rob's first top-20 finish in only his second year. Olie Linsdell, 20-year-old son of veteran campaigner Steve, moved up from the Manx and took creditable 18th and 20th places in the two Supersport races, and another MGP graduate, Sweden's Mats Nilsson, did even better by finishing eighth in the first 600 race, his TT debut. The feeling that the TT was in good hands was hard to ignore.

Billown's big day

So, we come to the postscript to TT 2008, and the controversial decision to stage two-stroke races at Billown and designate them TT races. How could 12 laps of the 4.25-mile course in the south of the island equate to three 37.75 laps of the Mountain Course? Was it right that someone could win three times round Billown and be ranked the equal of Carl Fogarty in TT terms?

I had some doubts as well, but there was another way of looking at it. TT legends like Carlo Ubbiali earned their success over the Clypse Course, and no-one thinks any the less of them. And why shouldn't riders who are experts with the smaller machines have the chance to shine?

Billown also gave us all a wonderful roll-over from the main races. It meant that wrapping up TT commentary from the Grandstand wasn't like falling off a cliff, as usual. After two weeks of living and breathing the event, it is always a massive anti-climax when it's all over. Billown solved all that.

The racing was brilliant, and there were no foul-ups from the commentator. The two TT races were given a heightened profile by having the riders switch off engines on arrival at the grid so Chris Kinley could conduct his usual last-minute interviews. Then they paraded round on a formation lap before reforming for the start. Roy Moore delivered passionate and colourful commentary from Cross Four Ways. After the race, Chris described the presentations which took place beyond my field of vision. The fanfare and the anthems were played as usual. With delightful symmetry, the first 125 TT at Billown was won by the last winner of a 125 TT on the Mountain Course, Chris Palmer. Ian Lougher won the Lightweight, his eighth TT win, and to put the pre-race debate into another context: how many TTs were Chris and Ian denied by the abolition of two-stroke racing around the mountain?

Billown brought down the curtain on what for me was my most comfortable TT so far. I felt at home in my role, and I thoroughly enjoyed it. I was the guest of Geraldine Jamieson, Manx Radio's leading interviewer, on her Sunday show, and was grilled on several aspects of my media life, including the challenge of following Peter Kneale and Geoff Cannell. I was pleased to be given the opportunity to state publicly that I did not see myself as a replacement for either of them. I told Geraldine that I was there to do the job to the best of my ability, but I could never replicate the immense knowledge of the TT that those two amassed through a lifetime's involvement.

Sadly, there was no opportunity for any of us in the Radio TT team to build on the renewed relationship with Geoff. Geoff, tragically, had died the previous September, a few weeks after discharging his duties as press officer at the Manx Grand Prix. His absence left a huge gap in the media centre in 2008, and a legacy which no-one who ever heard his broadcasts will ever forget.

2009 – Rossi earned huge credit for revising his diary

Play it again, Maurice!

A bombshell exploded shortly before TT 2009 when Maurice Mawdsley announced that he was retiring from the commentary box. With immediate effect.

This news came only weeks before the event. Maurice explained that he'd been thinking about it for some time, and decided that now was the time when he saw an American comedian performing on a cruise ship. Maurice had seen the same comic a couple of years before but this time he thought the guy was going downhill fast, and he didn't want to end up in the same situation. He didn't want anyone asking: "What's he doing still clinging on to his microphone?"

In fact, Maurice was still at the top of his game, and to quit so soon before the race was going to be a huge problem for Manx Radio. A replacement couldn't simply be whistled up with no notice. Happily for us all, Tim Glover persuaded Maurice to do one more TT. "It'll give us time to find a proper replacement and, just as important, it'll enable you to say a proper farewell." He also made a very good point that a lot of people would want to say a proper farewell to Maurice, which turned out to be 100 per cent accurate. It also turned out to be a 100 per cent exciting TT.

Practice Week was hot, and so was the pace. In Thursday practice, Cameron Donald smashed through the 131mph barrier. Thursday is, of course, the session when Radio TT usually has the full Outside Broadcast team in action, and Cameron's effort really whetted the appetite for what Race Week might produce.

There were plenty of bright moments as we waited for the serious action to start. Sidecar aces John Holden and Andy Winkle were spotted doing a lap of the course in a tuk tuk – one of those three-wheeled stink machines which serve as taxis in places like Bangkok. This one had been brought to the island by the Rotary Club after a fund-raising trek through the UK. The image of John hunched over the controls while Andy hung out of the side was wonderful.

As they passed the Bungalow they might, if the cloud of fumes allowed, have spotted a striking mural on the easterly face of the old motorcycle museum. This was a really impressive piece of work, full of sweeping lines and bright colours. It depicted a Honda motorbike with a rider wearing an Arai helmet, tearing across the landscape. The mural was the work of Australian Richie Knights, who had arrived on the island the previous December and set up a company called Artrageous Creations. I tracked him down via a mobile phone number which was just about discernible at the bottom of the painting. "I'm a mural painter and a sign writer, and I wanted to do something to make a mark and celebrate the TT," he told me. "I got in touch with Paul Phillips and we arranged to do this. The rider is based on Gary Johnson, and it obviously made a lot of sense to feature Honda because it's their 50th anniversary at the TT and Arai because it's the company's 25th anniversary."

It's remarkable how this small island exerts such an influence on people who have any kind of link to it. Richie comes from Perth, Western Australia, but has links with the island through his grandfather, who lived there in the '60s and '70s, and his sister who was living there in 2009. It had taken him two and a half weeks to complete the painting, which he'd finished on the Tuesday of Practice Week, the day before we found it.

Something else I discovered was the role that HM Prison Service plays in motorsport. Not something that I was aware of before, although clearly a lot of people in the paddock knew all about it. Admiring Paul Owen's substantial motorhome I was informed by his dad, Gareth, that the truck used to be a prison van.

"The prison service were selling off a number of these vans about four years ago," he said. "We had to go down to Kidderminster to get it. We paid £3200, and since then we've spent £3500 converting it. When we got it, it contained 14 cells and it had a pipe running the length of the truck for the prisoners to pee in. Quite a few motorsport teams have one, and rock groups too."

The 7.5-ton vehicle now provided sleeping space for seven, living quarters during the day, and a workshop for bike preparation. Gareth showed me round, and it looked great.

"The only problem is," confided Paul, "people see the truck and think we're minted. That's far from the case!"

Indeed it was, and Paul spent much of the fortnight trying to get the very last ounce of wear out of his somewhat understocked supply of tyres.

I was quite concerned about him but he proved what a capable rider he is by ending the week with his best-ever result on a big bike, steering his Team 98 Yamaha R1 to an impressive 13th place in the Senior.

The Radio TT team, sponsored that year by Sure Mobile, assembled for our official launch at the Villa Marina. Anthony Pugh, John Marsom (Manx Radio's Business Director) and Tim Glover briefed us on what to expect. Then the "best biking station in the world," to quote the jingle, was officially let loose on air, with Chris Kinley conducting a series of interviews with myself, other members of the team, and a number of riders who had come along to join in.

Among them was someone I particularly wanted to meet, listed in the official Race Guide as CR Gittere. How to pronounce the surname was the problem for the commentator. "It's Gitter-ee," he said, going on to explain what the 'CR' was all about.

"My name is Carroll Robert Gittere the Third," he announced. "My dad and granddad both had the same names. When I was brought up we all lived in the same house. Granddad was called Carroll, dad was Robert, so I ended up as CR."

I couldn't help feeling that CR looked a little out of his depth, and there's no denying that his early practice times were somewhat on the sluggish side. I wondered what his wife Jennifer would make of it all when she showed up a week later. But CR was made of the right stuff, and stuck to the task of learning the course. By the end of the fortnight he had three finishers medals out of three races. After his first, the Superbike TT, my wife Dorothy came across a somewhat embarrassed CR following the prize presentation, which he had missed. "I feel awful," he said. "I didn't realise you got a prize for finishing last!"

He also came up with a quote which immediately entered my Hall of Fame for great TT quotes. "The Catholics have Rome. We have this." Bless you, my son.

Another rider with a neat turn of phrase was at the Villa that evening. Mats Nilsson was having another tilt at the TT, despite having ridden only one event that year, the NW 200. For Mats, time management is both an art and a science. His commitments as head of a company which made water and air purification kit, as a property developer, as the inspiration behind the Troubleman clothing brand, and as a motorbike rider, were awesome. He was not exactly backward in endorsing his own ability. "If I had been racing full-time, I would have won a TT by now," he told me. It didn't sound like a boast – it was probably true. Mats divulged that this could be his last TT because of the lingering effects of a knee injury he'd sustained in a motocross crash at the age of 18. But he still added another great quote to my list: "I don't like bikes. It's the TT I like."

A newcomer called Jenny

Obvious ideas seem, well, obvious after you've thought of them. I don't know why it took six years for me to realise that it would be a smart idea to show up at the official briefing for newcomers, because this would make the business of meeting newcomers much easier. Oh well!

Gathering information on newcomers was always one of my priorities, and, until now, it had been somewhat hit and miss. I suppose that previously, on the first morning after arriving on the island, I was always busy finding my bearings and dealing with administrative tasks, and never thought about the newcomers briefing. It was not on any list of media opportunities and, so far as I know, no-one from the radio station had been along before. Certainly no-one had mentioned it. But this year I asked the clerk of the course, Eddie Nelson, if it would be okay for me to not just sit in but to go up front and introduce myself to the new riders. He agreed, and it was a useful move. I was able to hoover up a lot of detail about the new names, including Jenny Tinmouth, who was making her debut on the Mountain Course.

Jenny, from Ellesmere Port in my own neck of the woods, had originally entered 12 months earlier, planning to ride her 125 at Billown. But then she had upgraded to a 600 for the 2008 season so her first visit to the TT was postponed. Now here she was, with a Fireblade for the Superbike, Superstock and Senior, and a CBR600 for the two Supersport races. "I was brought up in a family of bikers so it never seemed unusual for me to be on a bike," she said.

What an impact she made. The first woman to enter a solo race since Fabienne Migout in 2004, she demolished Maria Costello's record as the fastest female with 116.483mph in the Superstock (and nudged it up to 116.835mph in the Senior). Admittedly the likes of Maria and another very quick lady, Carolynn Sells, were restricted to 750cc machines in the Manx Grand Prix, neither wanting to lose their MGP status, but for a rookie to go so fast, so confidently, so soon, was some achievement.

I bumped into Maria at the Billown TT races. "You must be fed up of questions about Jenny Tinmouth!" I said. "Not at all; Jenny has been fantastic," said Maria. Mind, she could afford to be magnanimous; she'd just been awarded the MBE for services to motorsport.

Of all the new names, James Vanderhaar was probably the unluckiest. After months of planning his trip from home in Washington DC he lost his sponsorship three days before his bikes were due to be shipped from the USA. His Yamaha R1 and R6 were still sitting in crates on the dockside. But bikes appeared, as they tend to do, this time with help from Robbie Silvester who produced a Kawasaki ZX10 and a Honda CBR600 to get the 29-year-old to the start line.

There was one significant non-change to the track in 2009. A new stretch of road had been built from the Nook to Governor's, running alongside the old road. But the riders would stick to the old road, which from now on would only be used as part of the race course. Tradition has never been something to be surrendered lightly at the TT.

The solo races in 2009 were magnificent. Competitive, compelling and ideal for a commentator. There was always something happening. Including the unexpected and the comical, both of which cropped up together on the first day of racing.

Now, I know we shouldn't smirk when the police cock-up, but when they do, and it's public, and it's live on air, well, you have to have a chuckle.

As usual, two police outriders preceded the deep blue limo of the Governor as it progressed regally down Glencrutchery Road on the first morning. The officers brought the little convoy to a smooth halt in the usual place, alongside the podium and directly in line with the commentary box. However, this year, the organisers had decided that the welcoming party of bigwigs would wait for His Excellency outside the hospitality village some 200 yards further along the road. So we had the wonderful sight of the Governor's car stopped with no-one to greet him, while the great and the good of the ACU, the Manx Government, and the Mayor and Mayoress of Douglas stood in line with no-one to greet. It was wonderful – except for those involved, of course. I was live on air, and I have to admit that I thoroughly enjoyed this terrific example of official buffoonery. The welcoming party, I observed, was looking like a jilted bride at the altar.

It seemed an age before the Governor's chauffeur, hero of the hour, jumped out of the car, tapped the motorbike bobby on the shoulder, and pointed out that they had guided the Queen's representative to the wrong place.

That gave us a good chuckle, but some of the other goings-on were beyond a joke. There was an unscheduled lap of the course by Philip McCallen, the former TT winner from Northern Ireland. None of us on the radio team had any idea that this was happening until McCallen appeared 45 minutes before the first race, leathered up and ready to go. I was furious about this because the one thing a host broadcaster requires is advance knowledge of anything which is likely to require live coverage.

The day was notable for the personal appearance of Valentino Rossi who was to garland the first three finishers in the Superbike TT. Again, it was my job to describe the ceremony: total farce. I called on the crowd to acknowledge the third-placed man, Guy Martin, and nothing happened. It took minutes for someone to get the word to Valentino that he was supposed to pick up the garland and place it around Guy's neck.

Eventually I was broadcasting instructions over the radio, piped through the course speakers, pleading with Guy to show Valentino what to do! I was able to make light of the tomfoolery by quipping that Valentino was clearly more used to receiving garlands than giving them out.

That would have been bad enough, but come the second race, the Sidecar TT, the same pantomime occurred again. This time it was a representative of the sponsor who seemed totally clueless when it came to performing the relatively simple task of placing garlands round the shoulders of successful sportsmen. It beggared belief and was totally embarrassing, as well as an insult to the riders.

It was tempting to send the whole thing up like Terry Wogan commentating on the Eurovision Song Contest. It was at times like that, though, that I was acutely aware of the dual nature of my role. As the commentator for people listening to the radio and online around the world I was one step removed from the organisation that runs the event, but when I clicked into the role of the official announcer for the ceremonies, I represented the ACU, the Isle of Man Tourism and Leisure Department, and all the various stakeholders, and slagging off their big show live on air would not be appropriate. So it's a thin line to tread.

The other thing that got me going that year was the inadequate information I was given by the Race Office. Right from the start in 2004 I'd been fighting what seemed like an annual battle to ensure that the Race Office communicated any changes in riders, numbers or machinery to me as soon as possible. It seemed an elementary thing to request, given the importance of my role, but every year there seemed to be problems. No sooner had I got the Race Office and the Press Officer to include me on the distribution list for the printed daily 'bulletins' than they brought in a new system which cut me out once more. This year the printed bulletins were axed. Instead, the changes were circulated on RaceMann, the TT's intranet, which was available to very few people – and I wasn't among them. "Okay, how do I get RaceMann?" I enquired. "Oh, it's on your terminals in the commentary box," came the reply. Except that the edition of RaceMann in the box didn't include the bulletins, and anyway, I needed the information well in advance of the races, not when the time came to go into the box.

The most important document for any commentator in any sport is the 'start list.' In football and similar sports it's called the team sheet. It's the final, official, list of competitors who will start the race, with their numbers and machinery, and in any sport it's the information that can be relied upon 100 per cent. But not this time. The list for the sidecar race included several entrants whose machines were produced by that noted engineering company TBA. These were machines which had practised on numerous occasions, been through scrutineering each time, and still

Continued on page 97

*John McGuinness, the
TT's Top Gun.
(Courtesy Alan Knight)*

*In the commentary box
with time-keeper Norman
Quayle.
(Courtesy
Dorothy Lambert)*

*Enter at your peril!
(Courtesy Dorothy Lambert)*

A view from a room: packed grid on Glencrutchery Road as the countdown to racing gathers pace. (Author's collection)

Barry and John Birdsall showed off this wheelchair-friendly trike in 2006. (Author's collection)

The trike caused much puzzlement at the Grandstand. (Author's collection)

Dan Clark (43), duelling with Dick Tapken (44), had his dad on board (see page 34) as well as his passenger! (Courtesy Alan Knight)

With Craig Atkinson after he won the Junior Manx Grand Prix by a mere hundredth of a second. (Courtesy Dorothy Lambert)

The Bolliger Kawasaki team made a colourful splash in 2007. Dorothy couldn't resist! (Author's collection)

Heike interviews Thomas Schoenfelder for our German listeners. (Courtesy Dorothy Lambert)

Radio TT 2007: (clockwise from left) Eunice Cubbon (producer), Mavis Brown (French commentary), Norman Quayle (timekeeper), Chris Kinley (pit-lane commentator), Tony Heron (engineer), Heike Perry (German commentator), CL, John McGuinness, Tim Glover (editor). (Courtesy Dorothy Lambert)

How to draw a crowd: McGuinness is in there somewhere after breaking the 130mph barrier. (Author's collection)

Everyone turned up for the Centenary TT. (Courtesy Dorothy Lambert)

Packing them in on Douglas Prom. (Author's collection)

Brammo was one of the first teams to compete in the zero-emissions TT. (Author's collection)

Chris Heath testing the Electric Motorsport bike at Jurby – but the real drama came on the podium. (Author's collection)

Dave Molyneux dealt with triumph and disaster. Here he is partnered by Patrick Farrance en route to another podium in 2013. (Courtesy Alan Knight)

Guy Martin brought star quality and a unique line in chat to the TT. (Courtesy Alan Knight)

Courage and concentration: no-one knows what's round the next corner. (Courtesy Alan Knight)

An inspiration to all sportsmen: Conor Cummins on the Milwaukee Yamaha at TT 2013. (Courtesy Alan Knight)

Jenny Tinmouth with her Guinness World Record certificates for her achievements in British Superbikes and the TT. (Courtesy Alan Knight)

Guy Martin finding a moment alone ... (Courtesy Alan Knight)

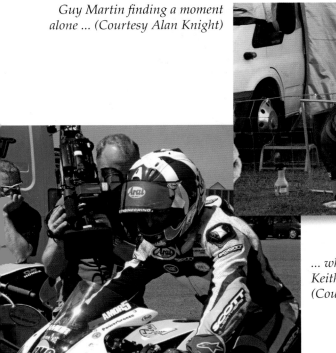

... which is not easy at the TT, as Keith Amor discovers. (Courtesy Alan Knight)

Australia's Cameron Donald, a winner on and off the track, takes Wilson Craig's Honda around the Gooseneck. (Courtesy Alan Knight)

Steve Mercer was an inspired choice to give the People's Bike its debut. (Author's collection)

The 'People' went road racing. (Author's collection)

Presenting the Yamaha Classic Parade on the Prom in 2011. (Courtesy Dorothy Lambert)

Interviewing one of Yamaha's best-ever racers, and my Radio TT colleague Charlie Williams. (Courtesy Dorothy Lambert)

The starting grid at Billown seen from 'The Best Commentary Position In The World.' (Courtesy Dorothy Lambert)

Finding out how it's done from Murray Walker. (Courtesy Dorothy Lambert)

Two bikes and a mountain. Gary Johnson and Guy Martin take on Snaefell as well as each other, 2011. (Courtesy Alan Knight)

Producer Eunice Cubbon ensures order prevails as I interview John McGuinness at TT 2011. (Courtesy Dorothy Lambert)

Collector's item. (Author's collection)

Rachael Clegg produced a TT souvenir in 2012. The calendar was not Rachael's only asset on view. (Author's collection)

Podium capers. Mark Miller (right) drenches his Segway MotoCzysz team-mate and 2012 TTZero winner Michael Rutter, while John McGuinness tries to take cover. (Author's collection)

Ian Hutchinson at Signpost Corner in 2012. Serious injuries prevented him building on his five-out-of-five in 2010. (Author's collection)

93

The Peter Kneale Media Centre. (Author's collection)

Radio TT voices in the Sure Studio beneath the Grandstand 2012 (from left): Roy Moore, Dave Christian, CL, and (conducting an interview) Charlie Williams. (Courtesy Dorothy Lambert)

Chatting to Maurice Mawdsley live on-air at Billown. (Courtesy Dorothy Lambert)

Debbie Barron, the first Manx woman to finish a Sidecar TT, with her passenger, Rob Lunt. (Author's collection)

There was an unpleasant undercurrent at TT 2012. (Author's collection)

Class act: Northern Ireland's Michael Dunlop on his way to victory in the 2013 Superstock TT. (Courtesy Alan Knight)

The eyes have it! Newcomer Chung Wai On from China greets the Mountain Course. (Courtesy Alan Knight)

Learning the course. Debutant Josh Brooks (Tyco Suzuki) follows John McGuinness (Honda TT Legends) through Kirk Michael in practice, 2013. (Courtesy Alan Knight)

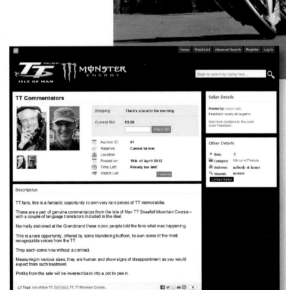

This item on the TT's auction site gave Charlie Williams and myself a good laugh! (Courtesy iomtt.com)

the official sources were saying they didn't know what kind of bike it was! When you see one or two obvious inaccuracies, you start to distrust the whole thing.

What this told me was not that the powers-that-be didn't think I was a priority. It told me that they didn't think the fans were a priority. I was only the conduit. The people who matter most are surely the customers – whether attending the races in person or investing their time and passion by following them from afar? They deserve to know who is riding what and with which number. If I didn't have the information, I couldn't relay it on.

At the same time Eunice had a problem because of the length of time it took Race Control to advise us of significant retirements when the race was under way. If a rider near the top of the field was late arriving at one of our commentary points, there was only so much padding we could do before we really needed to be telling the listeners what had happened. So, once the first day's action was over, we both complained to Simon Crellin, the press officer, and Simon decided we should air our complaints to Eddie Nelson. This we duly did in a meeting hastily convened in the Grandstand. Eddie was not in a sympathetic mood, and after a few minutes of unproductive conversation he got up and walked out. Not a great result!

Things did improve after that, though. Simon became very pro-active in supplying information, and we began accessing feedback about retirements from RaceMann. Which turned out to be a good system – once I was able to use it.

The Rossi Posse

It was the 50th anniversary of Honda's TT debut, and the Japanese company made a big commitment to ensure it marked the occasion in suitable style. Unlike '08, the factory team – as represented by Neil Tuxworth's HM Plant setup – was here in force, supplying the bikes and the deals for John McGuinness and Steve Plater. It was rewarded with a significant victory for each rider, and a new milestone in the ever-increasing pace of the outright lap record.

The drama started during that first big outside broadcast, our live coverage of Thursday's practice session. Cameron Donald took the Relentless Suzuki by TAS around the course at 131.457mph, 8.5 seconds inside McGuinness' record, the first time anyone had cracked the 131 mark, albeit unofficially. Twenty-four hours later Cameron's TT was over before it started, when he crashed at Keppel Gate and dislocated his shoulder. For the second time in three years he would be a frustrated absentee, unable to build on his sensational achievements of 2008.

The opening Saturday's programme was wiped out by rain, and

with the forecast unpromising for Sunday the two scheduled races were quickly rearranged for the Monday. At this point something quite amazing occurred. Valentino Rossi had been booked to visit on the Saturday, in company with Giacomo Agostini, the deal done through Dainese, which was again the leading sponsor of the TT. Most of us thought the postponement would scupper Rossi's visit, but the six-times Moto GP champion agreed to come on Monday instead. This was not the usual response of a superstar, and whatever the financial inducements Rossi earned huge credit for revising his diary at short notice.

Come the day, Rossi fans were out in force. From the commentary box I could hardly fail to notice them, resplendent in yellow sweatshirts and curly yellow wigs. I dubbed them the Rossi Posse, and the great man duly went over to greet them, creating the photo of the day.

The action was terrific, McGuinness setting a lap record on the first lap, breaking the outright record on the second at 130.442mph, and sealing his 15th TT victory in a race record time. Plater was second with Guy Martin third to make it a clean sweep for Honda which also took fourth and fifth places. Cameron's TAS team-mate Bruce Anstey dropped out with electrical trouble on lap one, a sign of things to come for the team, and other high profile retirements were Ryan Farquhar, Keith Amor and Conor Cummins. Dan Kneen, the local sensation of the Manx Grand Prix in 2008 when he made history by winning three races, finished an impressive 13th.

That set the style for the solo races. On Tuesday, the original programme from Monday was run but with the order reversed to give the Supersport teams more time before their second race on the Wednesday. Again, the first of the 600 races produced a Honda clean sweep, Ian Hutchinson winning from Martin and Amor. Records tumbled as Martin lowered the lap record on the opening circuit, and Anstey went round even faster on lap two. There were high profile casualties, too: Anstey pulling in at Brandywell with electrical problems when leading on the last lap, and Michael Dunlop bowing out early with a blown engine. Jenny Tinmouth chipped in with that record lap for a woman rider.

Hutchy did it again later in the day – it was 6.30pm when the Superstock started, due to more bad weather. There were no fewer than six changes of leader in a fabulous contest, with Amor, McGuinness, Martin, Hutchy, Martin again, and finally Hutchy again all taking over top spot – great for the commentators, and hopefully great for the listeners, too. Only after Glen Helen on the final lap did Hutchy finally get in front and stay there, leading Guy by just 1.2 seconds at Ramsey, but eventually taking it by nine seconds. It took a record-busting lap of 129.746 by Ian to shake off a very competitive field. Amor was third,

Plater fourth, and McGuinness fifth, which, weirdly, replicated exactly the top five in the earlier 600 race – and again, all on Honda machines.

That gave Hutchy two TT wins in a single day, and when we arrived in the tower on the Wednesday I was speculating that he could conceivably win three TTs in the space of 24 hours. Delays on the Tuesday had pushed both races back, but, if the second Supersport got away on time at 10.45, it could happen. The weather ensured that that piece of TT history remained in the imagination. In fact, the elements outdid themselves that day, as Maurice reported that hailstones were falling in the Glen Helen area! We were less than a fortnight away from midsummer's day. The start was repeatedly delayed, and we wondered what the record was for a gritter to get round the Mountain Course.

Eventually, Hubert Patricot, European President of Coca Cola, the owner of Relentless, flagged them away at 2pm in far from ideal conditions. The skies were clear but the roads were wet. Several riders didn't fancy it one bit, but Michael Dunlop did. Michael had had such a frustrating TT with mechanical problems that he had been close to calling it a day and going home, but now on his Streetsweep Marlow Construction Yamaha R6 he took the circuit by the throat and simply willed his way to victory. He was ten seconds up at the end of lap one, 14 seconds up by lap two, and continued to stretch the lead until he took the chequered flag with 31 seconds between him and Bruce Anstey. Conor Cummins on the McAdoo Kawasaki took third place for his first TT podium, a notable day for the island. For once Honda didn't get a look-in.

This was a great TT ride, and it was quite a moment to describe another victory for the Dunlop dynasty – a new generation of the old clan. But although the love of the sport may be in Michael's genes, his victory was a powerful combination of fine engineering, stubborn desire and pure talent.

Dead or alive?

Nicky Crowe and Mark Cox went into the first Sidecar TT as favourites to win. They had out-gunned Dave Molyneux and Dan Sayle in 2008, and, with a lap in excess of 116mph, were clearly the faster crew in practice. However, at the end of lap one they had a lead of only three seconds, and, when the first outfit passed Maurice on lap two, it was not Nicky but Moly. Nicky had been forced to retire at Greeba Bridge and now it was his fellow Manxman who was advancing his own hold on history. And he did it in superb style, racing ever more clear of a rapidly-dwindling field – John Holden and Andy Winkle retired at Black Dub, Gary Bryan at Cronk y Voddy, and Klaus Klaffenbock at Ramsey, all on lap two. It left Moly to win with ease in a new race record and capture his 14th TT title, equal to Mike Hailwood. Second place went to Phil Dongworth. It was his first TT podium, and Simon Neary also mounted the steps for the first time, in third. Both men had been knocking on the door for some considerable time and thoroughly deserved their moment. Tragically, Phil lost his life later that year at the Southern 100.

The three-wheeled events in 2009 were also overshadowed by an horrific crash involving Nicky and Mark in race two. It had been another day of delays. I dropped in on the team as they whiled away the afternoon in the paddock. Nicky's camp again looked very smart, with the topiary crow again on the wing. They were taking it easy and looked calm and relaxed. Steve Plater dropped in with some freebie sunglasses for the lads. And eventually, five hours late, they donned their leathers and lids and went to work.

At Glen Helen they led by 0.6 seconds from Molyneux with Dongworth third. Eagerly, we watched the computer screen for data from Ballaugh. No sign of Crowe and Cox. Other riders went through. It was obvious something was amiss, and the silence from Race Control made it worse. Times like this are anxious. When a rider is late arriving at the next transponder point it is always a worry, but that concern is magnified when no news of a retirement comes through. Then we heard that a machine was on fire at Ballacob, just before Ballaugh. Next, we received information that Nicky had retired. Then we saw a marshal run along the pit lane in front of our commentary point and pick up the red flag – though he kept it rolled up. There were no machines in our vicinity in any case. So now I was in that horrible position of fearing something terrible had happened, but not wanting to indulge in ill-informed speculation which would only make things worse. We needed concrete information, and for a very long time there was none.

We crossed to Roy who reported that John Holden led by seven seconds from Molyneux, with Tim Reeves third and Dongworth fourth. Then Roy spotted a red flag being displayed, and our worst fears appeared to be confirmed. The race was stopped. Reports filtered back to the Grandstand. Someone told Tim Glover that paramedics were treating Mark but had left Nicky in the road. That suggested only one thing, that Nicky was beyond help. That rumour, which turned out to be false, thankfully, hit me like a hammer, and it was difficult to keep going. I deliberately lowered the tone of the commentary – such as it was by now – because this was clearly no time for the usual hype and excitement. Maurice buzzed through to say that someone had told him that the crew had hit a rabbit in the road and had lost control as a result. I could hear all this in my headphones while talking about other things on the air. This rumour seemed fanciful and we didn't report it. It turned out to be true, although the animal was a hare not a rabbit. True it might have been, but we didn't know that at the time, and we were correct not to report it. Another report came in, saying that the boys were sitting up and thanking the marshals for looking after them. We were told by yet another source that the scene "looked like a war zone." I didn't relay any of that. The families of Nicky and Mark would be going through enough agony without hearing that sort of thing.

We gathered that only the first few machines had been able to negotiate their way around the wreckage of Nicky's LCR Honda. The bulk of the field was turned round and escorted back to Douglas by travelling marshals, the wrong way round the circuit. When they toured up to the Grandstand from St Ninian's it was a strange and sobering sight.

All this took quite some time and we still didn't know if the lads were alive or dead. My interpretation was that at least one was no longer with us. We watched the helicopter descend towards Noble's Hospital and, using binoculars, I could see the helipad through gaps in the trees. Two ambulances were on stand-by, which I took to be an optimistic sign: they wouldn't need an ambulance if one of them was dead. I saw stretchers emerge from the chopper and the ambulances move off very slowly on the short trip to the hospital, passing out of view behind the trees. There was no further news and we closed the show as quietly and decently as we could.

When I look back on that episode I wish I had at least been given the one piece of information we all needed: that they were both alive. Even if I hadn't been allowed to announce as much, the information would have informed the style of my commentary during those awkward moments. As it was, because I thought one at least had met his maker, I was preparing the radio audience for bad news simply by the style and tone of voice. In hindsight, it was inappropriate, although the reality was little cause for celebration, with both men sustaining a number of serious injuries which required lengthy treatment in England. Nicky didn't return to the island till the Manx Grand Prix was in progress that year, and Mark remained in hospital.

Electric drama

On a grey, windy morning at Jurby airfield a motorbike whirred into view, swept past the control tower and headed off on another lap. Silence, barely disturbed by the passing of the machine, settled again. Welcome to the world of green machines.

This was my first sight of an electric-powered racing motorcycle. Rob Barber on the Agni looked pretty smooth as he lapped the airfield. How he and the others would fare in the inaugural one-lap TTX GP was a topic of much debate in 2009.

The TTX machines were set up a separate paddock behind the newly-rebuilt pavilion in the middle of Noble's Park. They were a fascinating sight, some designed from scratch by their dedicated teams, while others used the chassis of a Suzuki or a Ducati; all powered by electric cells but with different styles of cells and different approaches to gearing and the recycling of energy. From the commentator's point of view, this was all new and needed a fair amount of research. I would have to describe the start and finish and ensure that listeners at home and around the course had enough detail to work out what was going on.

I spent a lot of time doing the good old journalistic thing of knocking on doors (or awnings) and asking questions. This, more than any other TT race, was more about the bikes than the riders, with all due respect to the likes of Thomas Montano and Mark Miller who were among the pilots. Among the interesting bit of information I picked up was that it was no coincidence that three of the teams were based in Oregon, USA. I discovered that the state government there had invested a lot of money in encouraging the development of alternative fuels, and that had attracted these companies to locate there. The presence of two teams from India was another positive step. At the time I was doing a lot of PR work for the Northwest Automotive Alliance in England, and, through that, I was well aware of the huge strides being made by the Indian automotive industry. I discovered that the Agni machine had been built in engineering guru Cedric Lynch's back garden, and the EVO machine had a chassis designed by former TT winner Peter Williams. Some of the bikes had been built as part of university projects, while others came from companies which already sold electric-powered scooters and wanted to go a lot further. Most of the machines had been assembled from scratch in a matter of months.

Despite the optimism of race organiser Azhar Hussain, and the backing of the FIM, motorcycling's world governing body, there were more than a few sceptics. Most of the press corps were sniffy about the whole enterprise. "They won't even complete a single lap in practice," said one reporter. One rumour had it that the start would be relocated to Ramsey, so that the bikes would encounter the mountain at the start of the lap, when their power was still strong, not towards the end. Others were scornful of machines that produced low speeds and no real noise. People moaned about the money the IOM Government had spent to support the scheme. I was genuinely surprised at the reaction. I thought that the TT was exactly the right place for this endeavour. After all, hadn't the origins of the TT been all about experimenting with new and developing technology? Where Rem Fowler and the internal combustion engine trod in 1907 was the same territory that Azhar Hussain and multi-cell lithium polymer batteries were going in 2009.

Practice proved that the bikes worked, and put up decent times – as Norman Quayle pointed out, many of them were faster through the Sulby speed trap than some of the sidecars! Rob Barber brought the Agni home to win the Pro class by a long distance, and Chris Heath took the American entry Electric Motorsport to first place in the Open class. It felt really good to be there and describe it.

There was one very tricky moment. This came as the riders gathered on the podium. Not for the first time, the podium ceremony proved to be a challenge! For some reason the top three from the Open class and the top three from the Pro class all went up together, instead of separately, which made the platform very crowded. Just as they got there, the official placings on my computer screen changed. There had been a whisper that Chris Heath would be disqualified for failing to observe the regulations under yellow flag, and now came official confirmation. Chris' name disappeared from the order, and Chris Petty and the Barefoot Motors team were promoted. It was one heck of a time for this to happen, with the riders all on parade and Chris waiting for his big moment. I had to make a snap decision – to proceed with the garlanding ceremony as per the riders on the podium, or to announce the disqualification. I couldn't allow the proceedings to go ahead on a falsehood, so I had no option but to announce the disqualification, and poor Chris had to make his way back down the spiral staircase. Later, after the ceremony, the organisers upheld an appeal against the disqualification and Chris was reinstated. For a while I felt that I had made a bad call, reacting too quickly to the change of data, but Eunice and Tim were adamant that I had been correct. I can only work from the information to hand and this was not a rumour, it was an official decision from the authorities. Okay, it was reversed later, but no-one in the commentary box was to know that. Despite that, I reckoned the inaugural TTXGP was a big success.

And so was The People's Bike. The idea was conceived by Eunice and her husband Mark, both heavily into all kinds of motorsport. They teamed up to win the Manx Rally Championship in 2008, Mark driving and Eunice navigating. The idea now was to invite members of the public to subscribe £50 to become part of a motorbike team. The concept was similar to that of a horse racing syndicate. I chipped in my 50 quid and became a team owner! The People's Bike was a Suzuki GSXR1000 supplied by Crooks of Barrow-in-Furness and ridden by a newcomer, Steve Mercer. Steve was an inspired choice. Not only did he take to the Mountain Course as if it was his local motorway, he was always bright and approachable. Steve finished 25th in the Superbike TT and 28th in the Superstock, the best newcomer each time, picking up two bronze replicas. The People were well pleased.

And so to the Senior TT, which provided us with elation, triumph, dismay and tragedy. McGuinness set another outright lap record and crossed the 131mph mark with a lap of 131.578 despite slowing for his pit stop. John looked to have the race in the bag, but on lap four his chain broke at Cruickshanks and that was that. Amazingly, Guy Martin went out for the same reason, his chain snapping as he set off from the pits for lap five when lying third. Steve Plater took over the lead and Conor Cummins was now second. Ian Hutchinson was third and on course for a £10,000 bonus as the first winner of the new points competition, spread over all five solo races, but he came off on oil at Quarterbridge on the last lap. Gary Johnson therefore completed the top three. Plater's win was further evidence of the extreme talent and versatility of the man, as I noted on air at the time – track, roads, endurance, whatever the occasion, Plater could master it.

And Conor's wonderful performance at TT '09 gave the island another home-grown hero to purr over, in tandem with Mark Cavendish who was doing great things on his pushbike that summer.

Tragedy reappeared with the news right at the end that unique adventurer John Crellin had crashed and died at Mountain Box on the fifth lap. How could life be so cruel? That same day John had fulfilled one of his lifetime ambitions by getting onto the podium at the TT, finishing third in the Open class of the TTXGP.

People with much less courage than John Crellin were making fortunes taking part in so-called extreme sports. John could put any of them to shame. An enthusiastic mountaineer, he had recently made his third attempt to climb Everest, beaten back by illness after reaching the final camp before the summit. That had led to a spell in hospital, and it was only a few weeks later that he signed on for the TT, 25 years after his debut. He rode all five solo races. Too much too soon after his illness? A number of people thought so, but John was never one for the easy option.

2009 was a memorable TT for Carl Rennie who grabbed a best-ever placing of fifth in the Senior at the age of 39, for John Burrows, tenth in the Superbike and eighth in the Senior on bikes entered by his own company Burrows Engineering, for James Hiller, ninth in the Senior for his first top-ten finish in only his second year, and for Dan Kneen who stepped up after winning three MGP races in '08 and took 13th, 11th and tenth in his first three TT races before crashing out at Black Dub in the second 600 race. Ian Mackman also got into the top-ten for the first time, tenth in the Senior in the PRF colours.

My own TT ended again at Billown. This year Maurice was available and looked after the commentary, with Roy at Cross Four Ways. I wanted to be involved in some capacity, but when Tim Glover asked me to replicate Chris Kinley's usual role of interviewing the riders on the grid just before the start I wasn't keen. I didn't have Chris' detailed knowledge, and I felt that I wouldn't do a good enough job. Chris was due to do paddock and post-race interviews. In the end Tim did the grid and I worked with Chris. I felt like a complete fish out of water, and it made me realise that the commentary box had become such a familiar setting that it was now my comfort zone. The nervousness I felt about doing these relatively routine interviews really surprised me. I'd done countless similar jobs in the past, but not for some time. Of course, once I got going it was fine and I even bagged a scoop when Dan Sayle revealed that he was quitting as a sidecar passenger to concentrate on his solo career. The retirement was one of the shortest on record because he accepted an offer to team up with Tim Reeves a few weeks later, but it was a good story at the time. Ian Lougher won both the Billown TTs, which were contested over two eight-lap legs. Ian thus took his tally to ten TT victories. A good way to mark the year in which he had completed a century of starts at the most famous motorbike races of them all.

2010 – The Honda coasted across the line and into Ian's own chapter of TT history

Old combatants

A couple of weeks before TT 2010 Dorothy and I attended a christening at HMS Eaglet, the shore base of the Royal Navy in Liverpool. The baby's dad was a part-time reservist. The old couple serving behind the bar looked fed up. The main focus after the christening ceremony was a party for the youngsters and no-one was buying booze. We got chatting to them and happened to mention what I'd be doing in a fortnight's time. The effect was dramatic and instantaneous, like a massive power surge.

Simply mentioning the TT brought the old fellow to life. His eyes began to sparkle, his face became animated and in no time an idle chat became animated conversation. Eric Wolfenden MBE was 83 and had been going to the TT since 1948. The shortage of customers at the bar was forgotten as he told me about his favourite spots from which to spectate, places he'd stayed, and his plans for this year. He and Stella were going over for the Senior, later than usual because of another engagement at HMS Eaglet. If ever there was a man in love with a sport, this was the guy. Equally important was what the sport was doing for Eric – and Stella. The TT was the highlight of the year – had been for 62 years, and was still working its magic.

There were changes in the Manx Radio set-up. The most significant one was that, for the first time in years, we knew – or rather, we thought – we would be providing radio coverage of the event for the foreseeable future. Over the winter the radio station had concluded negotiations with the IOM Government for a three-year contract, with a further three-year option, a satisfactory outcome to a challenge launched by my old mate Andy Wint on behalf of Energy FM, for whom Andy was now working. As it worked out, only the initial three years of the deal were completed, and the three-year option was set aside as a new contract was negotiated in time for 2013.

Maurice's successor at Glen Helen was Dave Christian, a Ramsey lad who did a fair amount of freelance sports reporting for Manx Radio, but no motorcycling until now. Manx Radio kept Dave's appointment under wraps until Practice Week when he was formally unveiled over the air (if such a thing is physically possible!) on Charlie Williams' morning *Chat Show*. There had been discussion as to whether Roy should switch from Ramsey to Glen Helen and Dave should move in at the Hairpin, but in the end it was a straight replacement with Roy staying put.

The other consequence of Maurice's retirement was that I was handed full responsibility for the commentaries at Billown – both the pre-TT Classic meeting and the post-TT races. This was great as far as I was concerned. It always took me a few days to adjust to being back in the TT bubble, and I figured the instant immersion in full-on commentary from Billown would shorten the process considerably!

As I anticipated, it was a really enjoyable experience. The Saturday contained only one race, with the rest of the afternoon given over to practice, so there was time to check out the runners and riders and take a swing through the paddock. I tracked down the legendary Bill Swallow, winner 14 times at these Classic races. Bill was again running the equally legendary Lawton Aermacchi which looked in superb nick. Mark Parrett was there too, and I seized the opportunity to ask why he hadn't entered the TT proper this year. Finance, was the reply. Mark was far from happy with the start money he'd been offered, and he'd also lost a fair amount of earnings from his job as an electrician in 2009 as a result of injuries picked up racing. He wasn't the only notable absentee this year – Craig Atkinson, Adam Barclay, Victor Gilmore and Mats Nilsson were all conspicuous by their absence, and Steve Plater was a high-profile absentee too, ruled out after breaking his arm in a crash at the NW 200. Gary Carswell was a reluctant spectator, having failed to recover from a crash in 2009 in time to pick up the required number of signatures on his Mountain Licence.

Compensation came from a number of riders moving up from the Manx, among them Scott Wilson who told me in the bar at the Mereside Hotel that one big reason for his switch was the weather. He was deadly serious. The 2009 Manx was afflicted by terrible weather, the monsoon turning the paddock into a quagmire. Scott was hoping for better conditions, and TT 2010 did not disappoint.

Another name missing from the TT grid was Martin Bullock, for over a decade the sponsor and inspiration behind a host of riders. In 2009 the Manx Grand Prix gave me another commentary highlight when one of Martin's riders, Carolynn Sells, became the first woman to win a solo race around the Mountain Course. Soon afterwards Martin announced that he was disbanding his team, and for a time it looked as if that would be the complete end of his involvement with the sport. Not so. He was still supporting Roy Richardson at the pre-TT Classic, and turned up in person as I was chatting to Dick Linton in Roy's awning. Martin told me he had set up a new operation, Martin Bullock Manxsport, which would enable him to support a variety of sports. He was no longer involved in the TT, but would still run a team, albeit a slimmed-down version, at the Manx. The MGP would be all the better for Martin's continued involvement.

The Saturday and a busy programme of racing on the Monday kept me busy. On the track the big story was Ted Fenwick's victory in the 250cc Singles. Ted was 82 years of age. Paul Coward raced against his son Jamie in the Post Classic, and it was quite a dice between the two till Dad retired on lap five, Jamie finishing second. Less enthralling was the sidecar race which produced just two finishers from a starting grid of seven; Vince and Phil Biggs the clear winners.

We had flames and smoke off the track as well when the IOM Steam Railway locomotive set fire to the cutting opposite the main stand. Officials and timekeepers from the Southern 100 Club piled out of the HQ to extinguish the fire.

One detail needed to be thought out – the handover from me to Charlie Williams, commentating at Cross Four Ways. I'd found this a hit-and-miss effort when I'd done Billown commentaries in the past, so this time I thought I'd better invest some brain action. Cross Four Ways is about two-thirds of the way round the course. For each race I checked the lap record time, then calculated two-thirds of that figure, knocked off another ten seconds to give Charlie time to clear his throat before the bikes appeared, and used that as my cue to hand over. The plan was that I'd start a stopwatch whenever the leading rider passed my point and hand over after the correct number of seconds – somewhere between a minute and a minute and a half. That was the theory but the plan collapsed because I kept forgetting to start the watch in the excitement of commentating on the leading bikes. The solution was to enlist the services of Dorothy who took on stopwatch duties. She started the watch each lap, and when the time came to hand over – remember that I was, of course, in full flow at this time – she would simply thump me on the back. Not very hi-tech but it worked brilliantly, and lap after lap we handed over at exactly the right time. What a team!

Hutchy's fabulous five

On the scale of 'most remarkable TTs' this was pretty close to the top. It wasn't just that Ian Hutchinson won all five solo races, which was as remarkable as you could possibly wish for, on the basis that it seemed impossible. No, this TT capped even that. It gave us an amazing series of very close finishes as, time after time I fired up the stopwatch to count the final splits second-by-second.

The achievements of Hutchy and his team stole everyone's thunder. The 30-year-old from Bingley rode for Clive Padgett's team in every race, on Honda machinery in every race, and each time the formula was a winner. Winning any TT is a remarkable achievement, and to take five wins out of five is something which would defy belief if those of us following the races in 2010 hadn't witnessed it at first hand. To win, everything has to be right – rider, motor, tyres, brakes, fuel, pit stops, those cheap components which can often prove irritatingly fallible, chains, and so on and so on. There's also luck. Success can stand or fall by what your rivals do, when you meet back markers, how many yellow flags are waved, etc. In 2010 ("twenty-ten, please chaps, not two thousand and ten," was Tim Glover's instruction) it all came right.

For me, the racing programme got off to an encouraging start when we opened our broadcasts on Saturday June 5th with a pre-recorded message from Geoff Corkish, the recently-installed Political Member for Tourism (the old political titles had been changed since 2009). I will admit here that in previous years I'd felt that one or two of the political figures who delivered a speech, live, before the start of racing rambled on a bit. Geoff was succinct, welcoming and businesslike, which is exactly what was needed. Then it was on with the build-up to the Superbike TT, which was extended by 15 minutes when the start was delayed by mist and low cloud. One delay led to another and another and it was eventually three and a half frustrating hours later that racing actually began – doubly frustrating because apart from the mist it was a gorgeous day. We stayed on the air for almost the whole of that delay, finding things to talk about from somewhere. Tim and Chris pulled off a terrific sequence of live radio, prowling round the Grandstand area finding interesting people to interview, 'throwing' to one another as each interview wrapped up. We heard from everyone, from the head of Suzuki to ITV presenter Craig Doyle. It was Manx Radio at its best – lively, unscripted, informal and entertaining. When we eventually came off air we had done nine and a half hours of non-stop, unscripted broadcasting, with just one 40-minute break when we handed back to the studio.

I speculated on air as to where in the world people were listening, over the internet. Immediately our little printer in the commentary box went over the limiter as emails and texts flooded in. These included emails from the Kennedy Space Center in Florida, the Johnson Space Center in Houston, and the British Antarctic Survey! We were also contacted from Orlando, Paris, Vietnam, many other worldwide locations, and also from Bruce Anstey's big sister in New Zealand! It just showed how the TT binds so many people together in their love of one unique sporting event.

This year the races were sponsored by Monster, the energy drink and competitor of Relentless. The Monster branding was prominent everywhere. There was a change of course car provider as well, with Corkills of Chester supplying a range of fabulous-looking Porsches. A couple of years earlier I'd done some corporate work with Corkills, whose MD, Manx-born Adrian Kermode, had assured me that I really could not afford NOT to have a Porsche, such was the marque's reliability and value retention. Alas, the reality remained that I really could NOT afford a Porsche, period!

It was Suzuki's 50th anniversary at the TT and Bruce Anstey on the Suzuki GSXR1000 of Relentless by TAS Racing had the number one plate. It was not to be a suitably memorable year for Suzuki, but Bruce's bike still looked great as it sped off the line to get TT 2010 up and running. John McGuinness was again the fancied rider in the big-bike events, but the bad luck which destroyed John's chances in the Senior 12 months previously was still lingering like the Manx mist. His race ended at Sulby on the opening lap, and when the leaders reached Ramsey it was local lad Conor Cummins on the McAdoo Kawasaki who was in front. Starting at 10, the 24-year-old Ramsey man already had a six-second lead from Hutchinson on the way to a phenomenal opening lap of 131.511mph, the fastest-ever from a standing start, and just six hundredths of a second off McGuinness' outright record.

Conor reeled off another 131mph lap on lap two, and, with a 21-second lead after lap four he was looking good. Then cruel fate intervened. The bike was reluctant to fire after the pit stop, and, although it struggled into life, there was clearly a problem and Conor's race ended with retirement at Laurel Bank. This propelled Hutchy into top spot and there he stayed, cruising home with a 33-second lead over Michael Dunlop, with Cameron Donald finishing strongly to claim the final podium place – two Hondas and a Suzuki. A good effort by Cameron, who dropped to 13th at one stage after overshooting at the Nook on the opening lap. It was obviously disappointing for Conor and John, but hard to begrudge Hutchy his first big-bike win. He had been consistently quick throughout practice.

One rider was less than pleased, though. Guy Martin was the first high-profile competitor to fall foul of the new speed restrictions in the pit lane. In 2010 the stop box was abolished and replaced by a mandatory 60km per hour limit. This was a good move: there had been some close calls in the pit lane the previous year. Once clear of the stop box bikes could run as fast as they wanted, and there was an accident waiting to happen. The organisers had trialled the new limit at the Manx GP and it had worked pretty well. Here the bikes would be equipped with limiters to take the guesswork out of it, but Guy was still picked up for speeding. That meant a time penalty of 30 seconds which relegated him from second to fourth in the final standings, an outcome which rankled with Guy for the next few days.

The official publications have told the story of that week more than adequately. There was a race, and Hutchy won. But only after some thrilling racing. On the Monday the first Supersport race was led by Guy Martin at Ramsey on lap one, and again by Guy at Glen Helen on lap two, but Hutchy took over by the halfway stage and won by three seconds, taking 18 seconds off the race record. Guy, Michael Dunlop and Keith Amor all beat the old lap record on the final lap, but to no avail, as Hutchy, having started at four, parked the bike on the return lane to await Guy's arrival at number eight before proceeding to the winner's enclosure. The afternoon saw the Superstock flagged away by former TT rider Mike Crellin, now working for race sponsor Royal London 360. This was a great scrap, and no-one was putting money on Hutchy to win as the action unfolded. It was Ryan Farquhar who dominated on his own KMR Kawasaki: six seconds ahead of Michael Dunlop at the end of lap one, eight seconds ahead of Hutchinson at the end of lap two when he relieved Hutchy of the lap record at 129.816mph. But Hutchy was brilliant over the mountain, and when they reached Ramsey Hairpin on the last lap with Ryan's lead reduced to 1.8 seconds the odds were shifting. Ryan gave it everything and I clicked the stopwatch as Hutchy blasted past the Grandstand. The Yorkshireman had started one minute and 20 seconds ahead of Ryan, and the tension reached new peaks as Ryan passed Cronk ny Mona with next to nothing to divide them. In the end the Ulsterman was just 1.3 seconds adrift after 150.9 miles, and it took a remarkable lap of 130.741 by Ian to beat him.

I was puzzled that day, having speculated at the start that we could be celebrating Honda's 150th TT win by teatime, when I was informed that Honda reckoned it was already at the 150 mark. My records stated 148. Having got back to base I looked into it and thought the discrepancy could be explained by the format of the TT races at Billown the previous year. The Lightweight and Ultra Lightweight TTs in '09 were both decided over two legs. The TT winner was calculated by the best aggregate performance of all the riders over the two legs. Hondas won both legs of the Lightweight (Lougher) and both legs of the Ultra Lightweight (Palmer and Lougher) but there was only one TT winner in each class – Lougher in both cases. For me, that equated to two wins for Honda, not four, so I didn't think Honda could count them as four separate victories. No doubt the historians will settle on an agreed solution, but so far as I'm concerned Honda was then on 150 wins, not 152.

Racing was postponed on the Wednesday, but not before I really feared we would see outright mutiny by the riders. It was a damp morning, and, as visibility showed little sign of improving, it was a surprise when Race Control announced that the second Supersport TT would go ahead. The track was wet, and this just did not seem like a good idea. At least two riders, Keith Amor and Guy Martin, declared they wouldn't race. Michael Dunlop was up for it, but not many shared his enthusiasm. In the meantime, we were having our own problems in the commentary box as the power cut out on four separate occasions. This, of course, cut off our output, and the broadcast had to be passed over temporarily to the studio at Manx Radio on Douglas Head. Under the circumstances it was no bad thing that the racing was postponed. There was no instant back-up from any stand-by source, so if this had occurred while the race was under way it would have been pretty awkward. The whole of the Grandstand was cut off, so presumably Race Control would have been affected as well.

The postponed action took place on the Thursday. Hutchy led for the first three laps, then Michael Dunlop seized the lead by a single second at Ballaugh on the fourth and final circuit. Michael was still in front when the bikes broke the transponder beam at the Bungalow but not by enough to hold off Hutchinson who again had a tense wait to see if he'd notched up the victory. By a margin of 1.4 seconds he had, with Michael second and Amor third. It was another race record.

The Senior confirmed Ian's five out of five, but again it was far from easy. The race was red flagged on the third lap when Martin crashed at Ballagarey. For us in the commentary box it was another of those occasions when the minutes seem to tick by very slowly. The red flag is always a worrying sight, and from our lofty perch in the tower we could see a column of smoke rising from the general direction of Ballagarey. Of course, I made no mention of the smoke, simply passing on the official word from Control that Guy had been involved in an incident. I discovered later that Guy's mum Rita had been spectating up at Keppel Gate and it had taken some time for her to make her way to the hospital where, thankfully, Guy was not too badly knocked about. The poor woman would have been worried enough without the commentator rabbiting on about columns of smoke.

It was indeed Guy's bike that was the cause of the fire, setting fire to a hedge. The fire service was called in to sort that out, then the race restarted as a four-lapper. At the time of the red flag McGuinness was in the lead by ten seconds from Hutchinson, with both Martin and

Cummins having been in top spot, McGuinness breaking the 131mph mark again, and both the Relentless boys, Anstey and Donald, retiring on the first lap.

Such is racing. Hutchinson took control second time around, leading from flag to flag, with two 131 laps in the first two – amazingly, Hutchy, McGuinness and Conor all exceeded 131 on the first lap. McGuinness went out at Glen Helen when the wiring to the kill switch broke, but, more seriously, Conor disappeared over the edge of the Veranda on lap three when only three seconds behind the leader. We were soon informed that he was conscious and talking to the marshals while waiting to be helicoptered to Noble's – good news, although it did rather gloss over Conor's actual physical state, as I was to discover much later. The race ended with Hutchy standing on the pegs as the Honda coasted across the line and into Ian's own chapter of TT history. Ryan Farquhar capped an excellent TT with second place, and Anstey, reprieved by the restart, was third.

Banishing the ghosts

The TT festival was much more fun in 2010. Whatever the powers-that-be had been thinking when they made Douglas Promenade a ghost town in 2009, there was a different mindset now. The funfair was back; street entertainment was back, and the island capital once again looked and sounded like somewhere you wanted to hang out.

There was a cost – these things don't come cheap – and part of the price seemed to be the TT races at Billown. After just two years of two-stroke TT racing in the south of the island the races were consigned to history, the money being spent elsewhere. You can't have it all, of course, and the return of the party atmosphere to Douglas obviously had to be funded somehow, but axing the Billown TT after just two years seemed premature. Two years is nothing in the context of TT history, and I thought the two-stroke races should have continued. It also seemed disrespectful to the riders who had contested the races there in '08 and '09 to bin them so soon. Having said that, I accept that the number of entries was not great, and I can understand that this would have been a factor. The partygoers and thrill-seekers were being catered for much better, though, and that's also part of the TT experience.

Among the many disparate individuals drawn to the island was an apparently naked man who found his way onto the grid at the start of the Superbike TT. In fact, he was wearing flesh-coloured leathers designed to resemble a naked male. The reason for this wasn't clear when I first spotted him from the commentary box, but the next day I met the character in Peel. He was Glenn Moorley, formerly a Peel resident but then based in London, and the leathers were part of a campaign to raise awareness of testicular cancer. Arai had fixed it for him to go on the grid and Yamaha UK provided a bike for him to tour the island. He told me he had two equally bold comrades – Mr Testicles and James Bum 002. I remembered seeing Mr Testicles parading round some football stadium, all part of a charity's mission to get men thinking about the risks of the various cancers to which they are prone.

The paddock looked better with more tarmac tracks, a legacy of the horrendous weather which had afflicted the MGP in '09. Manx Radio, for the second year, used one of the units under the Grandstand as a studio, and produced a lot more output from there this time – a very good move which made it much easier for the producers to get big names to drop by for interviews, compared to persuading them to go to Douglas Head.

From my perspective, the whole operation was smoother than ever before and that was because Simon Crellin was completely dialled in to what I needed. No longer did I feel that I was wading through treacle trying to obtain important information. I guess this was due to Simon having grown into his role and hopefully realising that I was not a threat but an ally. It also helped that under the terms of the new broadcast contract, Manx Radio was now 'official broadcast partner' of the TT. Information from Race Control arrived in a timely manner – even I was surprised when we were given so much detail about Guy's accident so soon. But information is crucial when there's such a risky sport as this taking place, the more so as individuals with mobile phones have the capacity to send messages, pictures and videos around the world in less time than it takes to read this sentence. Official information is vital to put those unofficial bulletins in context, and 2010 was a year when the organisers took that on board. Apart from the media interaction, things just seemed to be run better this year – no embarrassing cock-ups on the podium, for example.

Not that the whole fortnight went seamlessly. On the Monday of Race Week I was building up to the start of racing when there was a strange noise directly behind. I glanced round and saw Mavis stretched out on the floor. I was horrified. It looked like she'd passed out. I feared she had hit her head and knocked herself unconscious. The race was starting and I had to carry on. Fortunately, there were plenty of others who immediately responded. She had tripped and gone headlong, but thankfully suffered no damage – shaken but okay.

One strange phenomenon was the sight of a gigantic tent being erected in the heart of Noble's Park, and it was nothing to do with the TT. The monster was due to host a huge music festival soon after the TT, a descendant of the Peel Festival in Centenary Year. Many of my colleagues from Manx Radio were due to plunge straight into another hectic schedule of broadcasting on the festival as soon as the bikes departed.

The marquee occupied the space assigned to the electric bikes in '09. This year the green machines were back but it was all change, and not just in terms of the location of their paddock. In '09 the electric race was run by TTXGP, a separate company directed by Azhar Hussain. It was high profile and, as befits a debut event, there had been much pomp and circumstance. In the intervening months the TT had decided to organise the electric race itself, but who had decided what first was shrouded in mystery. The IOM Government released a statement saying that it had stepped in because the TTXGP company wouldn't commit to supporting the races in 2010, and instead had accepted an invitation to race in Paris on the same dates. I thought this was a shame, after everything the TT had done to welcome Azhar and promote his vision of zero emission competition. When I said as much on my blog I received a frosty response from Azhar, suggesting that the reality wasn't quite like that. But he didn't tell me what the reality was, so I was none the wiser.

This time the green bikes were quartered at the bottom of the paddock, and were not exactly easy for people to find. In any case, when I ventured down there to gather information for my commentary on the Wednesday of Practice Week there were only four teams in residence. They were in good spirits, though, and I caught up with some of the others at a team briefing in the Grandstand later.

Agni had two brand new Suzuki GSXR750 frames that year. SERT, a Swedish entrant, was using a Honda CBR600 frame, nicknamed the bike 'the bumblebee,' and had Mats Nilsson as part of the team. Ecolve expected to put road-going versions of its electric bike on sale in September of that year. Brunel had fitted a double motor instead of a single to the previous year's chassis. And Kingston University used the monocoque chassis developed (but not raced) by ex-TT rider Peter Williams in 2009.

HTBLAUVA again ran a machine developed by the Federal Institute of Technology in Vienna under the guidance of rider Martin Loicht. Martin pointed out that his preparations had been complicated by the change of administration. The TTXGP people had announced that in 2010 there would be a one-lap and a two-lap race, but when it disappeared (for whatever reason) the TT had reverted to 2009's one-lap race only, something that Martin wasn't aware of until March.

Of all of the machines the most bizarre was the Peace E Rider entry, by former TT rider Harald Gasse. Talking to Harald in his tent I was unaware that the bike he was discussing was the machine propped against the workbench. I'm sorry to admit that I thought it was a paddock scooter. Well, it did look like a paddock scooter. It was propelled by 6kW battery power and, said Harald disarmingly, "I'm sure it is the slowest bike here." He wasn't wrong, but Harald was not on the island to win races – he was there to spread his philosophy of zero emissions in a world of peace and love, straight from 1968 San Francisco.

MotoCzysz ("pronounce it sizz," Michael Czysz told me) had a chassis which enabled batteries to be changed in 30 seconds. Not that it needed to change the batteries, and MotoCzysz turned out to be a very impressive winner when the race took place.

New names in the chair

A few weeks after TT 2010, with the football World Cup and the Wimbledon tennis having been and gone, BBC Five Live asked its listeners which was the greatest sporting occasion among all the big worldwide events. The third caller to ring in nominated the Isle of Man TT Races, by which time the studio had already received at least two texts nominating the TT as well.

It set me thinking about what was the last sporting event which I'd found truly uplifting – something which had inspired emotions other than simple enjoyment. It was not, as I might have wished, the first football match to be played by the recently reformed Chester FC, the new version of the club I'd supported from boyhood. That match had sadly been tarnished by fighting among spectators. It was, I decided, the victory on the Mountain Course by Klaus Klaffenbock in the first of the Sidecar TTs that year.

Klaffi made his debut the same year that I made my mine for Manx Radio, 2004. He came with the status of a World Champion, someone who had proved himself among the good and the great. But he found the TT a different kettle of whatever fish they fry in Austria. Try as he might he couldn't crack it. In fact, more often than not, he was forced into premature retirement as others took the podium places. It must have been dispiriting for such a talented racer to be among the also-rans. But he kept coming back. Clearly the races had got under his skin.

In 2010 Klaffi was there again, this time with a significant change of passenger. Dan Sayle took over in the chair, having reversed his decision to retire from sidecars. The duo were not favourites – Dave Molyneux was fancied to win, especially with Nicky Crowe now retired.

The race got under way at 6.15pm on that first Saturday, three and a quarter hours late, and it was Klaffi who shot into the lead. It was, in fact, a start to finish victory, but that doesn't sum up the drama as Moly steadily closed him down over the last lap. Klaffi and Dan were ten seconds ahead at the start of that final circuit, but it was only eight seconds at Ramsey as the Manxman put in the quickest lap of the race. When Dave and Patrick Farrance, with plate one, crossed the line, it was again a case of clicking the stopwatch and waiting for the number four outfit to appear. Klaffi, with Daniel putting in an impressive shift all week as adviser, mentor, backside-kicker and passenger, held his nerve to win by 2.63 seconds after 113 miles of racing; a great moment!

The sidecars, as usual, provided their share of stories, starting in Practice Week. Newcomers Nicky Dukes and William Moralee broke down near Kirk Michael when the radiator cap flew off. Coasting into an unmanned petrol station they rooted through the bins round the back looking for a replacement, couldn't find one, and made their way back to the bike where they spotted the original cap sitting in the tray.

Matt Dix, another newcomer, was not the only newcomer in his family. I discovered that his wife Nicky was due to give birth in Noble's Hospital on the day of the first Sidecar TT, prompting me to speculate on air that Matt could become the first TT competitor to finish a race with a bigger family than when he started. In the event Nicky held on till that evening, when Sydnie weighed in at 9lb 2oz, dad having successfully completed the race with an average over 100mph less than five hours earlier.

The newcomers also included the Knight family – World Championship driver Gary made his IOM bow with son Dan in the chair. I met them at Brian Rostron's and it seemed that the prime mover in getting them over was young Dan. The Knights were a real dynasty. Gary had started in the chair for his own dad Eric, who was now supporting the younger generations, while mum Iris was also there, making sure that the family honour was upheld.

Race Two was, remarkably, won by Klaffenbock and Sayle once again. You wait seven years for a win and then ...

Sad days, strong characters

News that Paul Dobbs had died after crashing at Ballagarey in the second of the Supersport races arrived while we were still on air that day, Thursday June tenth. It was another crushing moment and I went home that evening feeling very low, despite witnessing Klaffi's second win and Hutchy's fourth that same day. I'd met Dobsy a couple of years earlier, and his delight in the world of bikes was instantly apparent, especially if the bike in question was a classic.

We didn't know at the time that the race also claimed the life of Martin Loicht. What a horrible irony. Martin was only riding the 600 races in order to qualify to ride his electric bike in the TT Zero. That news was handed to us in a printed statement soon after we went on air on the Friday, Senior race day. I looked at it and my heart sank. Heike was desperately upset. She knew Martin better than me. She did a terrific job to announce the sad news to our German-speaking listeners in a completely professional manner, and then went outside to deal with her personal shock, accompanied by Dorothy who is very good at saying and doing the right thing at times like that. Broadcasters are human beings too, and having to handle tasks like this is not easy.

At Billown for the Post TT Races I was asked to read out a statement from Dobsy's wife Bridget. It was heartbreaking, the way she talked of the challenges facing her and her two young daughters.

She also wrote, "We held nothing back in pursuing Dobsy's racing and so I need regret nothing. Our lives have been immeasurably enriched by the TT and the Isle of Man."

A couple of days after I returned home to Liverpool the phone rang. It was Bridget. She said there was to be a ceremony to remember Dobsy at the Grandstand. Would I, as she put it, compère the occasion?

I readily agreed. If she thought I could do something to help at such a time, I would certainly do so. But I will say now that it was difficult.

It was not really a memorial service. It was, to be blunt, Dobsy's funeral. And I was in the role of the minister.

There was little by way of a religious element to this. Instead, the outline of the service which Bridget emailed to me contained a couple of very short extracts from prayers, and the names of half a dozen people who were going to give their own personal tributes. The rest was down to me to fill in as I saw fit.

I felt humbled that I was being entrusted with this. And daunted. What should I do and say? The one thing that I absolutely had to do was ensure it went smoothly. A funeral is no time for mistakes and stumbles. And what should I say to reflect the mood of the occasion, to provide some sort of comfort without being too downbeat? Bridget wanted this to be a celebration, with people turning up wearing paddock jackets and team shirts, not black ties.

I put a lot of thought into these questions, and I hope I came up with the right words and the right balance. I thought through every aspect of the ceremony, from how I would start the proceedings to what I would do at the end. When the day came I was confident I would do what the family required, but still felt pretty edgy about it all.

It was a surreal day. I flew to the island from Liverpool that morning. I had plenty of time in hand before the 2pm service so I caught the bus from the airport into Douglas and called in at Mash, a café run by Dave Denteith, a TT and Billown marshal, and his family. Then I spent an hour and a half at one of the tables in the Sea Terminal, going over everything I planned to say and do. I bought some blank cards to write down the words. Then it struck me that there would be a microphone. Would it be on a stand, or hand-held? If hand-held, I wouldn't be able to shuffle the cards easily. It would look amateurish and clumsy. So I rewrote everything on a single sheet of A4 paper, so that I'd have no problems either way.

There was still plenty of time and I made my way from the Sea Terminal to Noble's Park on foot and grabbed some lunch at the café in the park. I didn't really want to associate with anyone – I just wanted to keep my focus and keep running over what lay ahead in case I'd forgotten anything.

I strolled up to the Grandstand at around 1.15. There were a lot of people there already. Tim Glover was there, like me in his Radio TT shirt. Manx Radio was very well represented. I met Bridget, the first time I had met her in person. I was struck by her courage and self-possession. It was astonishing. I was introduced to Dobsy's mum Dawn and his sister Shaylene. It was a lovely sunny day.

There were three microphones (all on stands). They were set up on the little podium which is usually placed on top of the platform in front of the Grandstand. The hearse arrived, carrying Dobsy's coffin, draped in the New Zealand flag, accompanied by his helmet. When I stood on the podium the coffin was to my right. A semi-circle of chairs in front of me were for the family. I couldn't look at the two little girls, Eadlin and Hillberry.

The ceremony went as well as it could. I won't recount it all but the script went out of the window at the start. It was such a lovely day, I simply opened the proceedings by remarking on that, and celebrating the fact that we were where we were, and that Paul had been who he was because he just loved racing down that road behind me. The script resurfaced of course. It was important to handle things correctly. My mouth, though, was as try as tinder, something I had never experienced before despite countless live radio, TV and public occasions. This was unique.

Back in Liverpool, I heard that Conor Cummins had been transferred to the Royal Liverpool University Hospital. We went in to see him. The lad had taken a proper battering. He had spent 11 hours in theatre having an operation on his back. His left arm was encased in plaster, held at right angles. Three metal rods were stabilising his left leg. Operations were still to come on the arm and leg, and they, we were advised, would be straightforward compared to the process of rebuilding his left knee. He was using an oxygen mask to help his breathing, and had a morphine drip to deaden the pain. This was the true price of a racing incident. This was the reality behind that brief bulletin telling the world that Conor was conscious and talking.

"He thought he'd fly to Laxey!" his mum Carol joked. The nearest and dearest need to be almost as brave as the riders.

Conor himself handled his spell of incapacity brilliantly. We called in several times while he was in Liverpool and he was always positive, composed and upbeat. A remarkable young sportsman.

So, TT 2010 had had a difficult postscript. The action itself, though, ended in typically encouraging fashion, with the Post TT meet at Billown dominated by William Dunlop and Roy Richardson. When I put down the microphone for the last time I was told that a couple of spectators were asking for me. I walked over the road and there, track-side, were Eric and Stella Wolfenden, TT stalwarts extraordinaire, adding 2010 to their incredible record of TT support, now stretching over eight decades.

2011 – "If anyone thinks you should call it a day, that's ridiculous"

Closer to the edge

Three motorbikes, as close in line as beads on a necklace, roared up the hill towards me. The noise was terrific, and atmospheric music projected the sensation into a new dimension. Not bad for a side-street off Piccadilly Circus.

This was the scene at the audio studios of Goldcrest, the film company made famous by its productions of *The Killing Fields*, *Gandhi*, and countless other superb movies. On this afternoon in February 2011 the place had been hired by CineMANX, the film company whose 3D cameras had been prominent at TT 2010. The film, *TT3D: Closer to the Edge*, was moving towards completion, and I'd been asked by the company to travel to London to record some new voiceover.

The brief was to recreate some of my commentary from the 2010 races. I'd already been informed that Radio TT's output was going to be used as part of the soundtrack. They now needed certain sections of the commentary to be re-recorded because parts of the original had the sounds of the bikes or the crowd at the wrong moments and they needed 'clean' audio to work with.

The audio facility itself was really impressive – spacious, dark, with a massive audio desk and a big screen on which the relevant sections of the film were projected. I was placed in front of a lectern holding my 'script' – some poor soul had had the unenviable task of transcribing the stuff that came straight off the top of my head on Senior Race Day eight months earlier. I was handed a lip mic, exactly the same type of microphone that I use at the TT, to replicate the quality of the audio. There was even a chair of exactly the same height as the one I use in the commentary, so the experience was as close to the real thing as possible. Not that I spent much time sitting down when I was commentating at the TT. I was nearly always standing up, and it was the same here.

Director Sam Southwick and her colleagues wanted me to reproduce not just the words, but also the mood of the original. That meant finding the right tone to match the words when talking about Conor Cummins going missing on the mountain, or Hutchy making history with his fifth win out of five. It was fascinating to see how they manipulated the commentary to match their pictures, which was where things diverged from the original. What I said was completely accurate, but the sights were not necessarily the same as those I would have been watching at the time. Which was fair enough, considering that all I ever saw on race day was that strip of tarmac down part of Glencrutchery Road. On the word from Sam, a bar animated across the screen, and when it reached a certain point that was my cue to rock into the commentary. The pictures were sensational, including that shot of the three bikes – and this was without any 3D effect.

I was impressed by the attention to detail that the company was putting into this enterprise. It wasn't only me who had been asked to reproduce some commentary, the island-based commentators had done something similar via a link from Douglas, some of which I caught while my stuff was being recorded. It was quite surreal to hear Roy Moore's voice talking about trouser-bulging excitement on the premises of the company that made *Gandhi*.

The film guaranteed that TT 2011 had a build-up like no other. It premièred in April with separate showings in London, Douglas and Belfast, and had an instant impact. The critics loved it. They applauded it for its honesty, for the highly individual characters, for the sensational pictures and the immense achievement of examining a high-risk sporting event, including its fatalities, and still creating a life-enhancing atmosphere. For all of that, producer Steve Christian, director Richard de Aragues and the whole production crew deserve massive credit, as do all those who agreed to let them into their precious space over TT 2010 – riders, families, teams, organisers and administrators. In no time it was being announced that *Closer to the Edge* had burst into the all-time top ten of documentary film releases worldwide.

The production company asked me to attend the Douglas première and introduce the film on stage. Dorothy and I flew over on the day and were given all the trimmings – limo and driver to meet us at the airport, a suite in the Sefton Hotel, and for me a place in the line-up at the top of the red carpet in the Palace Cinema to be presented to the new Governor of the Isle of Man, Adam Wood. It was all a lovely treat and we felt completely spoiled.

The only off-key note at the première came when the gentleman who was introducing the Governor to us 'VIPs' was seriously caught out. The line-up included John McGuinness, Guy Martin, Conor Cummins and Tim Reeves, but he didn't know who Keith Amor was and, most embarrassingly, had no idea who Bridget Dobbs was. Bridget of course is one of the stars of the movie, with her amazing strength of character lighting up the whole production as she reflects on life after Dobsy. The gent said something like, "Oh I don't know who this young lady is," so Bridget introduced herself and the Governor replied, "What's your involvement with the film?" He clearly hadn't been briefed, which was no fault of his but honestly, but what a cock-up!

My part in the formalities was to briefly introduce the film, which I did by predicting that it would become as much a part of TT folklore as *No Limit,* and then interview the leading characters on stage before introducing Richard and Steve. The full house was enraptured by the film and, when it went on general release, the ripples quickly spread.

Guy Martin was the main character in the film, and this, combined with his role in a BBC TV series called *The Boat That Guy Built,* introduced both him and the TT to a new audience. The TV series followed Guy as he renovated an old canal barge called Reckless using original processes from the Industrial Revolution. It was an interesting series, although I felt we needed a lot more from Guy himself if he was to become what the producers were presumably aiming for, the new Fred Dibnah. Be that as it may, the net result of both TV and film was that there was hardly a day throughout the spring of 2011 when the TT wasn't being talked about and promoted in some shape or form.

There was also plenty of interest in the activities of the leading players off-screen. The winter of 2010-11 saw an unusual amount of movement. Anstey and Donald both left Relentless, Bruce signing for Padgetts and Cameron for Wilson Craig, who was not retaining Guy. McGuinness and Amor remained with Honda but in a new guise, the Japanese company creating a new team, Honda TT Legends, to tackle the World Endurance Championship and some of the international road races. Eyebrows raised when Guy signed for Relentless, a highly corporate team which didn't look a natural home for a maverick. Ryan Farquhar was busy building up his own KMR team, signing Sandor Bitter for the TT and Adrian Archibald for the Irish roads. Michael Dunlop worked out an arrangement with Paul Bird's World Superbike outfit to ride the new Kawasaki ZX10 in the big-bike races.

By this time the biggest deal of the off-season had been finalised: Ian Hutchinson signing for Shaun Muir Racing, Shaun having done a deal with Yamaha to provide the bikes. I felt this instantly threw any predictions for 2011 out of kilter. Padgetts' bikes were proven, and the team worked brilliantly. Yamaha is a great name at the TT, but, in 2011, it was on the crest of a trough. The R6 was a contender but the R1 was totally off the radar. So Hutchy did not appear to have taken a step forward, in sporting terms anyway. As it turned out we didn't get to find out because Ian sadly failed to recover from serious injuries sustained at Silverstone the previous September.

Two weeks before everyone congregated on the island the NW 200 was ruined by a combination of bad weather, a bomb threat, and an oil spill. That prevented the teams from getting vital time on the bikes – except the Honda TT Legends who were busy reeling off the miles in the Endurance Championship. It seemed that everything was pointing towards a successful TT for McGuinness.

Looking good, smelling great

A big highlight of 2011 was our refurbished commentary box at the TT Grandstand. It had got pretty manky over the years, with ancient equipment, wobbly stools, and scruffy paintwork. The problem was, Manx Radio didn't think it made sense to refurbish the place when it only had one- or two-year contracts from the IOM Government to cover the races. Now that it had a longer contract there was more incentive, and many thanks went to engineer Bob Allison who took responsibility for bringing about improvements. We had a new mixing desk, new talk-back system, new laptops, new stools, a fresh coat of paint on the walls, and also an air-con system. Bob even fixed up one of those aerosol devices which puff out a squirt of scented air every 15 minutes. Roy Moore wasn't impressed. Next time he was live from Ramsey he pointed out that in his commentary box there were two fellas who could also puff out a squirt of odour every 15 minutes.

One of the great things about working at the TT as a journalist is that you can talk one-on-one to the top people without having to fight your way through a labyrinth of PR merchants and spin doctors. Football used to be like this, and is poorer (spiritually if not financially) for the change.

One afternoon in Practice Week I spent a fascinating 40 minutes in conversation with Wilson Craig, whose profile rocketed in the wake of the *TT3D* movie, and was now – for the first time – running two riders: Cameron Donald and William Dunlop. It's safe to say that Wilson was enjoying TT 2011 rather more than he did the 2010 event. There was a really positive vibe about his camp, and it wasn't just in the camp where good judges were mentioning Cameron's name as a rider who was really 'on it' that year. Cameron himself breezed in wearing a woolly hat and looking relaxed. Not long afterwards he set the fastest time of the night in the Supersports at a speed of 125.110. Both Cameron and William were on identical equipment. Cam's superbike was the machine that was built for Guy Martin to ride at the 2010 Ulster GP, replacing the one that disappeared in flames at Ballagarey.

In the McAdoo awning chief engineer Marc Cooper showed me some of the adjustments he'd had to make to accommodate the rebuilt Conor Cummins. The pegs, usually in line, had been offset because Conor couldn't bend his left knee as much as he used to, and the bars were built up to compensate for a loss of flexibility in Conor's back. The fact that Conor was here at all was a major miracle, not just for surviving the crash at the Veranda the previous year, but for coming through massive surgery and getting himself back to fitness. The adaptation of his bikes underlined what an effort it had been.

Marc, like Wilson, was happy to give his time to this journalistic enquirer, which to me emphasises the spirit and commitment of this unique sport – less a sport, more a lifestyle. Conor had a new superbike and new superstocker that year, plus the previous year's ZX6R.

I also spent some time in the Honda truck where Adrian Gorst gave me the low-down on the Honda TT Legends' kit. The bikes dated back to 2008, and had their last major upgrade in 2009. The engineering team here was drawn from the crews that worked with Honda's endurance squad and the BSB squad. Adrian looked after Ryuichi Kiyonari's bike in BSB and Keith Amor's bike here. John's bike was the responsibility of Chris Pike, who also oversaw Shakey Byrne's BSB Fireblade. A couple of days later I caught up with Clive Padgett. I wanted to know if Anstey was on the same bikes that Hutchy rode to five wins, and learned that the bikes were all new this year. Clive also said he would have run both Bruce and Hutchy if Hutchy hadn't moved on.

In my blog a few weeks pre-TT I predicted that the Honda TT Legends would win both superbike races, and, on air at the Radio TT launch, I predicted that John McGuinness would win the first of them and set a new lap record in the process. Not completely accurate! The lap record remained intact, but the rest of my prognoses were spot-on. Another of my predictions was that, in direct contrast to 2010, we would have a different winner for every race, and only John's success in the Senior, doubling up his win in the Superbike TT, spoiled that.

TT 2011 was unpredictable and very controversial. We even got off to a prompt start in dry, sunny conditions on the first race day. It was great stuff. McGuinness, Anstey, Gary Johnson and Martin all lapped in excess of 130mph on the first lap. Lap two saw Anstey grab the lead, with both him and John upping the ante to 131mph. But Bruce retired at Quarry Bends on lap three and Guy was out at Hillberry on lap five, leaving John to take the win by 56 seconds from Cameron Donald.

I was disappointed for Bruce and Guy. It was soul-destroying for them both to have to retire and it meant we didn't really get the close racing I was expecting. Equally in the sidecars, Klaffi and Dan Sayle had worked out what it took to win, and, from Glen Helen on lap one, there was little doubt about the outcome.

In the commentary box it was a good long day's work, over seven hours, but I have to admit that I really loved those long stints. You are concentrating, involved, for hours on end, and afterwards, if things go well, you feel as if you've done a decent shift. The funniest moment came at the end of the sidecar race. I checked my notes to see if Dave Molyneux's race record had been broken and saw that it hadn't. At that moment Norman Quayle held up a scribbled note which said "a new race record." I was speaking live on air at the time and the message perplexed me because Norman doesn't get his facts wrong. I was still wondering how to deal with this when he put the message down in front of me, as he did so removing his thumb from the word "Not," which he had written at the start of the message!

Monday wasn't so good. A crash at Gorse Lea on lap two took the life of Derek Brien, one of the heroes of that amazing Manx Junior Grand Prix in 2006. The race was restarted and won by Anstey, with a final lap, which, under different circumstances, would have been warmly remembered by everyone present. Bruce was four seconds adrift of joint leaders Gary Johnson and Cameron Donald at the start of the third and final lap, and won it by eight seconds from Keith Amor. Cameron retired at Kirk Michael on the last lap, a cruel blow after he had led by 20 seconds from Amor when the red flag came out.

Later that day Michael Dunlop secured his second TT victory by taking the Kawasaki ZX10 to the winner's enclosure in the Superstock race, having led from Glen Helen on lap two. McGuinness was second and Martin third, each having led for a spell on the first lap. But the day was dominated by the incident involving Derek Brien. That evening I posted this on the blog:

"Five years ago I had one of the most uplifting experiences in all my time as a radio commentator. It was when Craig Atkinson and Derek Brien duelled wheel-to-wheel in the Manx Junior Grand Prix before Craig edged it by one hundredth of a second. It was the closest finish ever around the Mountain Course, and to call the two riders home was a real adrenaline rush – not bad when all you're doing is standing up holding a microphone!

"Today in the same commentary box on the same Mountain Course I had to report the death of one of those great racers, Derek Brien. We don't yet know the full circumstances, but Derek crashed at Gorse Lea, just before Ballacraine, and was declared dead shortly afterwards. When the red flags came out it was horrible, but then last year's Senior was red flagged because of Guy Martin's crash at Ballagarey, and he escaped with relatively minor injuries. Not this time. In the commentary box we were handed a printed statement from the ACU announcing Derek's death around ten minutes before the race – the 600cc Supersport – was to be restarted. We took the decision not to read it out until the race was under way. We felt it would be horrendously insensitive to read out this news at that moment, knowing that the PA system was relaying our broadcasts, so the riders would hear the news just as they were setting off. We knew that other radio stations and websites would not delay, but at Radio TT we were in a different situation and I believe we made the responsible decision.

"The riders found out soon after they finished, but not before the podium ceremony had gone ahead as usual with the champagne being sprayed. In the press conference the winner, Bruce Anstey, apologised for what might have been seen as a lack of respect, explaining that he simply hadn't been given the information. I still think it was correct that we didn't relay the news before the race. Perhaps he should have been informed before the garlanding, but knowing the right time to break serious news is not an exact science.

"We received an email from someone asking how we could sleep at night, knowing that someone had been killed but we'd carried on as usual. Well, we did carry on, although not as usual. It is quite difficult to be the bearer of bad news and then get on with the rest of the broadcast. However, one thing I think is important is that as a presenter you have to be professional, and that means you don't become over-emotional. It does no-one any good if the presenter is breaking down. If there is bad news, report it with clarity and respect, and like anyone else, get on with your job.

"Bridget Dobbs sums it up in the *TT3D* film. You can't love the death and you can't love the loss, but you can't love the event without knowing that death and loss are an intrinsic part of it.

"Derek Brien's greatest triumph for me was the sportsmanlike way he accepted his defeat in that sensational race against Craig Atkinson. 'Aka' was the man we were all talking about, but not so many would have been doing so if Derek hadn't given him the race of his life. Twelve months later Derek came back to the island and won the Manx Junior Grand Prix himself.

"So today has been a day that only the Isle of Man can serve up. We have seen victories for the old fella, Bruce Anstey (42), and the young gun Michael Dunlop (23). We have had long delays, champagne celebrations and a few laughs. And we have lost a good man and a good racer. None of these is cancelled out by any of the others. It's the mix, it's the event, it's the challenge. It isn't all roses, but it is what it is."

"Stop whingeing"

Come Wednesday, people were pretty jumpy. The second Supersport race was delayed for nearly two hours because of rain. It was another of those occasions when we felt the riders were coming under pressure from the race authorities to put their lives at risk. When it was announced that the race would start despite a lot of damp patches, four of the top riders said they didn't want to race. They started anyway. At Radio TT we received an email from a listener who said that she hated listening to the commentary because of the anxiety in the voices of Dave Christian and Roy Moore; clearly both commentators fearing accidents were inevitable. We were barely into lap two when rain returned and the red flags came out. By this time Mark Parrett had come off at Laurel Bank, while, at Union Mills, there was a nasty moment when Amor crashed and Martin and Donald almost came to grief at the same time, Guy hanging on somehow as the bike tried everything to part company with him. McGuinness, sitting behind the three of them, could see the water spilling off their tyres and knew things were about to take a turn for the worse. We were horribly close to a major tragedy from which the TT might have struggled to recover.

The following day nerves were still raw despite much improved weather conditions. On lap two at Ramsey the red flag appeared once again, immediately reported by Roy. Five riders promptly pulled in. At Union Mills at the southern end of the track a flag marshal heard the broadcast and showed the red flag as Amor, Donald and Martin sped by. But it was all in error. The flag at Ramsey should not have appeared and the marshal at Union Mills responded to the radio report instead of waiting for official word from Race Control. The race continued and the main beneficiary was Gary Johnson. Gary had pulled out of the original race 24 hours earlier on lap one, an electrical fault to blame, but this time he was in complete command on the East Coast Racing Honda, leading from flag to flag to win by eight seconds from McGuinness, John snatching second place when Donald retired at Signpost on the last lap.

Controversy continued to boil. Senior raceday offered what was by now a familiar script. Rain had left puddles across the track in the north of the island. Again there was pressure on the riders to get the show on the road, but the word from those who took part in the Milestones of the Mountain parade lap was that it was nowhere near safe enough for racing. The right decision was made to delay the Senior until 5.15pm, but not before we'd been heading towards mutiny once again. With 20 minutes to go we were still on for the scheduled start. It was representations from the riders which brought common sense to bear. John McGuinness spoke to Control by phone, and only then did Eddie Nelson agree to the postponement. I thought too much responsibility was being placed on John's shoulders by the riders in general. Chris Kinley interviewed several of them, and virtually all said that they would take their lead from John. I'm not saying that was a bad idea, it clearly wasn't, but one man shouldn't have been left in such an exposed position, taking such responsibility. I thought the leading riders should form a committee which would jointly make recommendations like this, or the TT Riders Association should be more pro-active.

Eddie Nelson had previously been in a spot of bother when he apparently told the marshals to "stop whingeing," when there were complaints about the length of time it was taking to get them down off the mountain during Practice Week. Threats of mutiny abounded yet again. Tempers cooled after Eddie went on Radio TT to apologise, but the mere fact that he felt obliged to make this gesture spoke volumes for the resentment among the troops. I didn't have a lot to do with Eddie directly, but he didn't strike me as the sort of guy who would readily agree to a public apology. At times he could be OK to deal with; at others he was somewhat abrasive. It wasn't a shock when it was announced shortly after the TT that he was standing down as clerk of the course. I never got the impression that he relished the role.

As for the racing, the Senior, run on dry roads, produced another superb race. Guy went off like a rocket on the Relentless machine, lapped at 131.038 and led after two laps. By Ramsey on lap three it was McGuinness in front and that's how it stayed, with John notching 131.248 on lap four en route to his 17th TT win in a new race record time, with Guy second and Bruce third.

There were no really close finishes in 2011, but there was certainly drama in the second Sidecar TT. Klaffi and Dan had reprised their smooth form of 2010 to take the first race, and it looked like it would be the same again when the duo led by 16 seconds after two laps. But John Holden and Andy Winkle cut the deficit to six seconds at the Hairpin on lap three as Klaffi struggled with a machine suffering from a broken water clip. We had a TV crew from Austria in the commentary box, filming for a report on Klaus. The script didn't go according to plan. By the time the data came in from the Bungalow we knew we would be greeting a new winner, and so it proved, John and Andy coasting home a clear 45 seconds ahead of Conrad Harrison and Mike Aylott. Tony Elmer and Darren Marshall took third place for their first podium as Klaffi eventually made it home in sixth place.

That second Sidecar TT produced one of the moments that makes the TT special. Robin Daykin, aged 74, and his wife Annette, 60, were among the entrants. Robin broke his neck two years earlier in a crash at the Tonfanau course in North Wales. Later he broke his back. He had also been diagnosed with cancer, with which he seemed to be dealing incredibly well. It certainly hadn't diminished his zest for life. "When you get older you've got to get your priorities right," he told me. "You've done your bit for your country, paid your taxes, been in the forces; you've done your bit for your family, and if anyone thinks you should then call it a day, that's ridiculous."

Robin last competed on the Mountain Course in the Manx Grand Prix on a solo in 1957. Since then he'd continued to compete elsewhere, switching to sidecars in 2004. He'd bought his current outfit two years previously from fellow TT driver Wayne Lockey. Not that racing had been the whole of Robin's life. Far from it. "By trade I'm an electrical engineer, but over the years I've done everything from selling bibles on the doorstep to running a croft." He also became a dad for the first time at the age of 50. I asked what had given him most pleasure in this incredibly varied life, outside family events. "Catching my first salmon – it was 14lb, on the River Esk in Scotland. Equalling the lap record at Tonfanau last year. And getting third in the Czech Classic Championship."

That was before he won a finisher's medal in the second Sidecar TT, having failed to qualify for the first. His celebrations matched John Holden's.

A final word on the racing, and it goes by the name of John Burrows. John rode in the Electric TT, won by Michael Rutter for MotoCzysz. John's bike gave up near the end, and we had the incongruous sight of cutting-edge technology relying on one man's grit to complete the challenge as John pushed in from Governors to take sixth place. The bike, inappropriately enough, was called the Lightning.

Murray Walker

I remember 2011 as the year I got to meet Murray Walker. Murray was one of the star guests that year, and made the Milestones of the Mountain parade – marking the centenary of the Mountain Course – a big success. As the riders came to the line I handed to Murray who was positioned on Glencrutchery Road, right by the starter. His role was to commentate on the machines leaving the line, and this he did with typical warmth and emotion. It helped that the parade was very well organised, which wasn't always the case with previous parade laps. Murray also had the bonus of some excellent research by freelance journalist Phil Wain, who had prepared detailed notes for him. The riders appeared in the correct order, one by one, and waited for Murray to give us the run-down, then set off. It meant the spectators in the Grandstand got proper information, and the riders and machines were treated with proper respect. Up till then, every parade lap I'd seen around the Mountain Course had been a free-for-all, with scant opportunity to identify individual machines or give the public a proper service.

Murray came up into the commentary box which was a real buzz. I'd never met him before, and was really pleased to have the chance to do so. We chatted about the system he and his dad Graham used to estimate when the riders would reach the various commentary points. The commentary team would meet in the Sefton Hotel on the eve of the race and discuss who were the likely front runners and what speeds they were expected to produce. They would then calculate the probable splits and do their best to hand over at the right time. Murray explained that the task was made harder by the starting numbers being allocated at random, so a favoured rider could well start near the back of the grid.

This was also the year I was asked to take on additional work outside the races. I was booked to be master of ceremonies at a posh dinner on the evening of the Senior TT, and shortly before the races I was also asked to present two events on Douglas Promenade during Race Week. The first was a parade by the Classic Yamaha team run by Dutchman Ferry Brouwer. The second, the next day, was a version of the Milestones parade. These didn't quite go as expected. Tickets for the dinner were priced very high and didn't sell. The event was cancelled. With the parades on the prom, there seemed to be a gap in the chain when we had a planning meeting because no-one from the TT organisation was there, and when the event time came no-one was there either. It was left to me and the riders to sort it out between us at the last minute, but there was plenty of goodwill in evidence and we got it all sorted without fuss. I have to admit that that isn't the way I like to go about things. Some people are brilliant at broadcasting by the seat of the pants, but I prefer to know what to expect, as far as possible, so I can prepare accordingly. Still, I had to accept that no-one really knew what was going to happen till it happened, so you just have to go with the flow. The Milestones of the Mountain parade included Charlie Williams, Luigi Taveri, Mick Grant, Dave Roper and Nick Jefferies, all former TT winners who have played their part in shaping this great event. The most moving for me was Nick, who represented his legendary nephew David by riding the Yamaha R1 which DJ rode when he became the first rider to crack the 125mph barrier for a lap in 2000. Nick was wearing DJ's own leathers, which created an uncanny illusion that we were really seeing DJ in action.

The joker in the pack was an unscheduled addition to the display, Graham Hardy, who turned up riding his version of the legendary Shuttleworth Snap, the fictional creation of George Formby in the film *No Limit*. Graham and his pal Jem Fraser explained to me beforehand that they had a little comedy routine which they could perform if required. I told them to go ahead. This turned out to involve stealing my cap, replacing it with a wig on my head that made me look like Freddie Boswell from the TV show *Bread*, and doing a magic trick in which Jem pushed two red handkerchiefs into my jacket and, when he extracted them, out came a white bra! I have no idea how he did it. Good knockabout stuff which gave everyone a laugh.

Afterwards there was a sensational display of stunt riding which left everyone awestruck. It wasn't just on the Mountain Course where the two-wheeled action was memorable that year!

When I looked back over the events of the fortnight, the name which gave me most cause for celebration was that of Simon Andrews. For a newcomer to take 11th place in the Senior with a fastest lap of 125mph was amazing. The Mountain Course is no pushover, and Simon put down a serious marker for the future with his efforts in 2011. It was all the more impressive given that everything seemed to go wrong in Practice Week, by the end of which Simon was so disillusioned he was tweeting that he would treat the rest of the TT simply as preparation for the next BSB meeting at Knockhill.

This was a year when the TT Points Championship had some meaning, after being rendered totally predictable in 2010 by Hutchy's clean sweep. McGuinness was the winner, but Keith Amor's achievement in taking second place despite not winning a race showed how consistent he had been, and that's what the Championship is there for. I was pleased to see Ian Mackman win the Privateers Championship, and repeated in my blog a comment I made in commentary, that I couldn't see the logic in banning Mackman from the next year's Championship because he was successful this time. The rules stated that if a rider finished in the top-ten of a race one year, he or she couldn't qualify for the Privateers Championship the next. So long as he or she was still a privateer, why-ever not? It seemed unreasonable to penalise a rider for his own success. Theoretically, Ian could have finished ninth in one race, not finished any of the others, not won the title, but be banned from being considered next time.

By this time I'd developed a good, solid system for handling these immensely complex live broadcasts. The basic essentials were: be accurate, be up-to-the-minute, give a sense of occasion, reflect the traditions. The next layer of requirements were: try to be entertaining, have a laugh when possible, include and give credit to the whole radio team, be as comprehensive as possible (in no other event, I think, would I even want to announce the entire list of finishers in a very long race, but at the TT and MGP, every finisher achieves something immense).

My system included a database on every single rider and sidecar crew. If you broadcast live, you cannot know who will make the news, and there's no time to look up background info if someone unexpectedly does something special. You need to have it in advance. So, throughout the year I would update my records with info like riders' achievements at non-TT meetings, changes of team, new sponsorship deals, personal and family news, etc. Of course, I never used the vast majority of it – but no commentator ever knows what you are going to need, so you do the lot and know you are covered. In the build-up to each year's TT (and MGP) I'd bring all my individual records up to date, including each rider's comprehensive TT or MGP results. I laid them out so that the information I was most likely to need was most prominent: age, birthplace, home town, best TT results, fastest lap speed, last year's results. After that, the data could go on and on. By the time I finished, the likes of McGuinness, Martin and Farquhar occupied several pages. I'd print out every sheet and have the lot in front of me in the commentary box, ready to be plucked from the file as soon as needed.

I developed my own lap charts that enabled me to record the information in a format that allowed me to keep track of the race, and also have the details quickly available to report and recap. My other vital piece of paperwork was the race sheet, a single sheet which had the vital statistics for each race: title, sponsor, distance in kilometres as well as miles, lap and race records, last year's winner, notes about the trophy, and any unusual facts from previous runnings of that race.

I could go on and on about the technicalities of commentating on a TT race but to give an idea of them I'll restrict myself to this one example. The end of a race is tricky because you only have about 1.5 seconds between the winning rider coming into your view and then passing the chequered flag. That doesn't give you enough time to build up to the big finale, describe the scene, and react to the thrill of the moment. So you have to be talking about the winning rider for a good 30 seconds before he or she, or they (sidecars!), come into view. In the box we'd see the transponder tell us when the leader passed Cronk ny Mona (approximately one minute to the finish), and by 2011 we also got an added signal when they reached Governor's (approximately 30 seconds to go). From that moment I would usually talk about nothing other than that leading rider so that when they sprinted out from behind the trees alongside the rugby field I could seamlessly (well, that was the idea) pick up the real commentary and hit the high note at the very moment the chequered flag waved.

One rider whose data was not required in 2011 was CR Gittere, the American rider who had competed over the previous two years but wasn't here this time. But he still grabbed the last word of that year's TT. CR emailed from his home in Charlotte, USA. "I am sitting here with a six-pack of beer in the hedges outside of my house with head phones on listening to Radio TT on my iPhone. My neighbours keep given me funny looks. Apparently they just don't get it." Brilliant!

2012 – We don't need the World Anti Doping Agency – they really do go that fast

The end of the Manx Grand Prix?

There was a terrific boost in the build-up to the 2012 TT when Manx Radio was short-listed for one of the industry's top awards for our TT coverage. IRN (Independent Radio News) has annual awards to recognise the best output by commercial radio stations across Britain, and among the three nominations for the Best Sports Story was us! The show which caught their eye was the one featuring the second Supersport race in 2011, when the riders had been close to rebellion as they were ordered to race despite wet conditions. The judges were clearly impressed by the way we had handled that dramatic situation, and I am sure it was Chris Kinley's ability to get the riders to talk about what they really thought, and feared, which made the biggest impression. In the event the prize went to the Midlands station BRMB for its coverage of Birmingham City's victory in the 2011 Carling Cup Final. But simply being short-listed was a big deal. I was really surprised and quite hacked off that Manx Radio didn't invite either me or Eunice to the big presentation in London. I've been involved in a few of these big broadcast bashes over the years, and I've never known a radio station not invite the presenter and producer. Whether they're staff or freelance, it makes no difference. As it happened I would have struggled to go anyway because of work commitments 'up North,' but Eunice should definitely have been there. After three decades as producer in the tower she deserved recognition.

The whole business of the award was played down when we all assembled for the start of the 2012 event. As usual there was a 'welcome' meeting in the Sure Studio beneath the Grandstand, and I was expecting the team to receive a pat on the back for the nomination; but there was nothing. And when it came to the broadcasts, the only person who mentioned the IRN nomination, to the best of my knowledge, was me!

The radio station really missed a trick there, and I think it has done that a few times over the years. It didn't seem to 'big up' its own achievements and personalities enough. If you visited the Manx Radio website any time over the years I'm covering in this book, you wouldn't find much by way of news, pictures or audio about Radio TT. Yet the radio station's coverage of the TT means so much to so many people. I thought it should have a permanent section on the website devoted to Radio TT, with pictures and features on the big names, like Peter Kneale, Geoff Cannell and Maurice Mawdsley, something about the history of the radio service, latest news, and, of course, recordings of the great races.

I decided to fill part of that gap by developing my blog (charlielambert.wordpress.com) so that anyone could check out pictures of the people whose voices they heard, like Mavis and Heike, and also the people who work so hard without being on-air, like Eunice, Norman Quayle, and the engineers.

For an all-too-brief year, it looked like Manx Radio had the answer. Before TT 2012 it launched the website manxradiott365.com, offering a great selection of race commentaries, plus music. Dan Walker ran the site for the radio station, and the aim was to turn it into a money-making operation. It deserved to succeed, but unfortunately it was wound up in April 2013 amid recriminations between Manx Radio and the Manx Government over funding for the site after commercial sponsorship and advertising failed to materialise. Even then, manxradiott365.com didn't include information about the history of the service or any profiles of the contributors. And once it had gone, the priceless archive commentaries vanished from view, instead of being transferred to Manx's main website.

The real source of discontent at TT 2012, however, was the future of the Manx Grand Prix.

In the spring of 2012, the Department of Economic Development's chief executive, Colin Kniveton, told *Motorcycle News* of plans to drastically cut back the MGP, with fewer classes and fewer races. This was not well received by the Manx Motorcycle Club, which, after all, ran the races, and hadn't agreed any such thing, or by large numbers of road race fans. At Billown, campaigners were selling T-shirts with 'Save the MGP' on them, and there was a terrible air of anger and frustration around the place. The weather for the classic racing was glorious, and the racing was gripping, but the sub-plot was impossible to ignore. I quickly lost count of the number of people who told me how unhappy they were.

This was down to two things. One, the threat to the MGP races, and two, the feeling that the dedication of countless volunteers was being taken for granted. The DED seemingly wanted to turn the Manx into an event for classic races only, and do away with the modern races, effectively chopping the event in half. It was so disappointing to see all this. Road racing is meant to be fun and the people who keep the wheels moving are in it for the enjoyment, but that seemed to be in short supply. Everyone looked grim.

I couldn't quite understand where the DED was coming from. I could understand if the MGP was under threat from insurers, or from safety campaigners, or from Manx residents who were fed up with road closures, but why was it being attacked by the island's own Department of Economic Development? A little bell was ringing in my head. Hadn't there been a survey quite recently which showed that the MGP made a financial profit for the island? I trawled through my records and quickly uncovered a report commissioned by the island's Department of Tourism and Leisure, in association with the Treasury's Economic Affairs Division, which showed that in 2009 the MGP contributed £4.9 million to the island's economy, including income of approximately £800,000 to the IOM Government. So far as I could see, there had been no research to update those figures, so why, if the event was making a decent profit, was anyone trying to emasculate it?

At the radio team's 'welcome' meeting, there was a bit of debate about how we should handle this. My view was that the MGP row was manna from heaven to us as broadcasters and journalists, and if that's what people wanted to talk about on the chat show or via emails during the commentaries, then we should facilitate the discussion. As it turned out, it was largely academic because the TT took over, Charlie Williams received hardly any calls on the chat show about the Manx, and the subject didn't crop up during the raceday commentaries. But that wasn't the end of the matter. The day after the 'welcome' meeting, Charlie and I were invited to a meeting with the officials from the DED. Full of curiosity, we turned up at the DED's HQ in Upper Church Street. We were introduced to Trevor Hussey, the department's director of motorsport, and Heather Smallwood, who had headed up a research project into the future of the MGP. Over 90 minutes we were given a detailed presentation, revealing the results of surveys, focus groups and questionnaires. The outcome was interesting. The figures confirmed what I thought – that the event was profitable and making a net contribution to the IOM Government. But they had identified several threats to the medium and long-term health of the MGP. Two were particularly significant: the age profile of those attending the Manx was getting older, and there was an increasing number of classic motorsport events in the UK which could be seen as rivals. This was very interesting, and serious, and I thought the DED had a good point in deciding that something had to be done to attract younger people, and to prevent the 'classic pound' being spent at places like Cholmondeley and Goodwood instead of Douglas.

The trouble was, those sections of their argument had been largely overlooked, and one big reason was the premature way that changes to the MGP programme had been announced without the MMCC being on board. Trevor accepted that. He also agreed with my view that, whatever happened, the DED had to mend fences with the MMCC or there would be no MGP in any format, and possibly no TT either. No road racing on the island could go ahead without the volunteers who fill posts from race control to admin to medical to marshalling and countless more, and if the DED didn't adopt a more friendly approach it was in serious danger of sabotaging everything.

I wrote on my blog that all sides needed to swallow some pride, and predicted that after the TT the DED would invite the MMCC to resume talks about the event. And so it proved, with agreement being reached to run the Classic TT on the first weekend of the traditional MGP event, with a big promotional effort to attract new support, and the modern races to follow. And all over the usual duration that has stood the test of time. A sensible outcome all round. But one that, possibly, was costly in my case.

Olympic rings

This was, of course, the wonderful year of the London Olympics and the stardust of the five interlocking rings spread throughout the British Isles. At one stage there was talk of the Olympic torch being carried round the TT course in a sidecar, but, unfortunately, it didn't happen. My only glimpse of the flame came a few weeks later when I went back to my birthplace, Windermere in Cumbria, to see the torch coming down the lake on one of the old steamers that I remember from my childhood. Despite typically miserable Lake District weather it was quite emotional, but what I'd really been hoping for was to commentate on the flame passing the TT Grandstand. As it turned out, the schedule only allowed for a short section of the course to witness the torch relay; World Enduro Champion David Knight carrying the torch (whilst on the pillion seat of a bike piloted by Milky Quayle) from Quarterbridge to Braddan.

I opened our live session by declaring that the TT redefined the famous Olympic motto Citius, Altius, Fortius (Faster, Higher, Stronger), and added, "We don't need the World Anti Doping Agency here – these guys really do go that fast, and it's all entirely legal." My ex-BBC pal Graham Fazackerley, sound recordist at all my visits to the TT in my TV days, texted: "Nice to get a bit of Latin in the TT commentary!" Some people thrive on culture.

The organisers tried hard to incorporate the Olympic spirit, with Olympic high jumper Ben Challenger invited to bestow the garlands at the end of the Superbike TT. Continuing where he left off in 2011, it was John McGuinness who received the laurels as the victor. It wasn't quite a flag-to-flag win, as Cameron led at the Bungalow on lap one, but all the other transponder points showed John in front. In a Honda one-two-three he won by a comfortable 14.88 seconds from Cameron, with Bruce Anstey third.

If that was relatively straightforward, the rest of the day was not. The sidecar grid lacked Klaus Klaffenbock, now retired, while the previous winner, John Holden, retired at Glen Helen on lap one. Dave Molyneux pounced like the vigilant fox he is, snapping up his 15th TT victory, and giving Patrick Farrance his first – Patrick, a picture of ecstasy as they crossed the line, and rightly so. This was another bit of history, as Dave gave Kawasaki its first ever Sidecar TT win, and also became the first competitor on either three or two wheels to win with engines from all four leading Japanese marques. Ben and Tom Birchall were second, laying down a marker for the future, with Conrad Harrison and Mike Aylott completing the line-up in the winners' enclosure.

So far so good. But then ... too much hanging around for everyone. The schedule should have segued smoothly into a practice session for the solos followed by the first qualifying lap for the electric bikes. Instead, it was over an hour and a half before the solos got going, and, as the weather closed in, the green bikes never got their lap at all. The reason was a parade lap for just four bikes, which, frankly, stretched the forbearance of spectators, competitors and marshals a bit far. The riders included former Olympic 400 metre runner Derek Redmond (of the Splitlath-Redmond team) and Ben Challenger, while one bike was turned out in memory of Mark Buckley who tragically was killed at the NW 200. The memorial to Mark, a great guy as well as a magnificent supporter of road racing on the island, was fair enough, and gave some credibility to the thing, but at a cost of too much hanging around for everyone. I know the event thrives on publicity, and a column in a national newspaper about one guy's lap of the TT course is good value, but I thought the balance was wrong here, and said as much on the blog.

That first day belonged to the seasoned campaigners, Molyneux and McGuinness, and, come the Superstock race on Monday afternoon, it was McGuinness all over again. Considering he had never won it before he made it look pretty easy, never threatened after seeing off the early challenge of Ryan Farquhar who held the lead briefly on lap one. John won it by 7.8 seconds from Michael Dunlop who produced the fastest lap of the race, 129.253, to take second, with Ryan third. As the top three made their way up the spiral staircase to the podium I had the pleasure of describing a garlanding ceremony carried out by one of my former students, Merita Taylor, in her role as marketing manager of race sponsor Royal London 360. I always knew she'd do well.

For drama, there was nothing to beat the first of the Supersport races. The pulse quickens in the commentary box when we expect a close finish, and it was certainly beating away merrily as that one neared its conclusion. From the moment Michel Dunlop retired at Ballig on lap three, the race was up for grabs. At that point Michael had an advantage of 21 seconds, having led from the start, but now it was Gary Johnson in front, with Cameron Donald and Bruce Anstey close behind. As they sped down Glencrutchery Road at the end of lap three Johnson was two seconds ahead of Anstey; Anstey was 0.2 seconds ahead of Donald – nothing in it. At Dave Christian's post Anstey had halved the gap and at Roy's lookout he was just 0.4 seconds behind Gary, with Cameron still just 0.2 seconds behind. The top three, bunched to within little over half a second. Over the mountain they came and I double-checked that my stopwatch was working. But now Johnson was fading fast, out of fuel as it transpired, and at Cronk ny Mona Anstey had the lead from Donald but still by less than a second. Donald had plate number four, Anstey plate number five. They'd started ten seconds apart. Cameron's Honda in the Wilson Craig colours screamed out of the trees fringing the rugby pitch. He crossed the line and I jabbed the stopwatch. Now Bruce had to finish in less than ten seconds to take the win. Over the air I counted down the seconds. Here came the Padgett's Honda. Again I jabbed the stopwatch. 9.3 seconds! Bruce had done it – by 0.7 seconds! I declared Anstey the winner and almost immediately the computer confirmed as much – 0.77 to be exact. Great moment, and not just in the Padgett camp. It was a terrific feeling in the commentary box as well – tingling emotion at the sheer excitement of the moment, and elation that we'd called a tight result spot on.

The race had been delayed for over two hours (a fatal accident involving a biker was the tragic cause) and as a result of that delay we were on air, give or take, for ten hours that day, a marathon even by Radio TT standards. The 150 miles of racing had come down to just 0.77 seconds; a matter of a few yards. It wasn't quite as close as Craig Atkinson's famous win over Derek Brien in the Manx, but still a fabulous finale, and just what I enjoy in the special context of this time-trial racing around the Mountain Course.

Anstey is a phenomenon. Well into his forties, and, by his own admission, not much of a racer outside the international road races, he moves unobtrusively through the paddock, materialising like the

Cheshire Cat, no-one quite sure where he came from. But what a talent, and what strength of mind. Every year there's a standing joke about Bruce's sleepiness, but there's a reason for this, the legacy of his diagnosis with testicular cancer in the mid-1990s. At race time, he's as sharp as a tack and still full of ambition to win races. This was his ninth TT win and his 24th podium. In fact, he was only denied a quarter-century of podiums by another ridiculously slender margin, 0.01 seconds separating him from third-placed Ryan Farquhar in the second Supersport race.

That wasn't such a clear-cut moment in the commentary box. Bruce was again number five, Ryan number two. We also had the winner, Michael Dunlop, and runner-up Cameron Donald to worry about, so I relied on the computerised time-keeping for the battle for third and fourth. The instantaneous data told me Ryan had grabbed third but then came a brief moment of confusion when another section of the timing display indicated both riders as having the same race time – thus, a dead heat. It was soon resolved as per the original flash, in Ryan's favour. Meanwhile, the Dunlop name was top of the leader board from start to finish. William led at Glen Helen on lap one, but retired at Kirk Michael; then Michael took over and completed his third TT win, a great way to mark ten years as a road racer.

Right people in right places

My battle to get the right information at the right time hit a new obstacle in 2012. Someone in the hierarchy decided to abolish the system of bulletins – these used to be circulated to all officials and me as the commentator whenever a rider changed his or her number or bike, or withdrew from the event, and so on. In 2012 there was very little official information, which left far too much to chance. Not knowing what was going on in the paddock made it impossible for us to update our information in advance of the races.

That was bad enough, but come race day, we discovered that the information available on the start lists had also been pruned back. Until 2012 we had a good system in which, on the morning of the race, a list would be produced with the name and number of each rider, their entrant/sponsor, and the make and capacity of their bike (sidecars manufactured by TBA excepted!). It was exactly what we needed.

But that year, the new-style start lists missed out much of that vital information. What we got was rider, number, and start position. We did not get confirmation of bike, entrant and sponsor. Instead we got a repeat of the details that applied in Practice Week – which was fine in the majority of cases, but if a rider had changed bike, we would be none the wiser. This was ridiculous, and, in my view, short-changed the fans again. If a leading rider had a change of bike we would know about it anyway, but with riders outside the top dozen it was an information lottery. I had to trust that all riders were still on the machines they rode a week earlier in practice. Which was fairly unlikely.

After the TT I complained in writing and made three constructive suggestions for the future. Well, they were intended to be constructive, and I can only hope they were received as such since I never received any feedback as to whether they had been considered. One: all rider withdrawals to be notified to accredited media as soon as they are known, and a final definitive list of withdrawals or non-appearances to be made available after everyone has signed on. Two: the bulletin system or something like it to be reinstated so that commentators would know what changes had taken place as soon as possible. Three: proper start lists providing key information – rider, number, start position, bike, entrant/sponsor, all correct and up to date, and all in one place. It didn't seem too much to ask.

Anyway, back to the action. Even without the practice lap on the Saturday, the electric bikes provided us with genuine drama and excitement come the day of their race, the Wednesday. The £10,000 prize for the first 100mph lap looked likely to be cashed in this year, with MotoCzysz having upped its game, and McGuinness making his debut aboard the Mugen Shinden. Mugen has close ties with Honda, and wasn't here just to make up the numbers. John looked a picture in white leathers with a lighting flash motif.

The complication with the electric bikes is that you can't always predict how any machine will finish, even with two thirds of the race gone. A rider who appears off the pace at Ramsey may well have conserved enough of that precious energy to make huge inroads up the mountain, while conversely, a hare at the Hairpin may resemble a tortoise with batteries low at the Bungalow. Getting under way mid-afternoon, with damp patches on the track and showers threatening, it looked like Michael Rutter as the MotoCzysz rider led McGuinness by 37 seconds at Glen Helen and 53 seconds at Ramsey, but McGuinness had power in hand and more than halved the deficit over the mountain. It wasn't enough, though, as Michael crossed the line in 21 minutes 45.33 seconds, an average speed of 104.056mph, also becoming the first rider to win the zero-emissions race twice. John and third-placed Mark Miller on the second MotoCzysz also broke the 100 mark, with Rob Barber the only other finisher. A race of attrition among the lower ranks, but more history was made by the top brass.

The second sidecar race was a good scrap, with Molyneux, Birchall and Tim Reeves all taking the lead. Tim, with Dan Sayle in the chair as a late replacement for Dips Chauhan, was six seconds ahead of Moly early in lap two, but when it mattered Molyneux and Farrance produced a lap of 114.486mph to win by 17 seconds. Debbie Barron became the first Manx woman driver to finish a Sidecar TT, one more to keep the statisticians happy.

And another first in 2012 was the inaugural running of a TT race for 650cc 'Supertwin' bikes. This was another example of a successful initiative by the Manx Grand Prix being picked up by the TT, and, in the heated atmosphere of that year, it was a useful rejoinder to those who wanted to reduce the MGP to a classics-only event. The TT race was given the Lightweight branding, and a new trophy was commissioned. As commentator I needed some information about this new trophy so that I had some relevant facts when it appeared in public for the first time. It's all about knowing the right people in the right places at the right time, and I quickly located Lloyd Mister from G4S, guardian and protector of the TT treasure chest. Not only did he give me the info I needed – the trophy had been made by BDG of Birmingham – he produced it from his hideaway in the paddock and I was able to have my photo taken with it before it had even been presented to the first winner. It's a sizeable and stylish piece of work, with a lovely miniature version of the famous Senior trophy, Mercury on the winged wheel, mounted on the top.

The Supertwin class had been soaring in popularity on the roads, with Suzuki's SV650 and Kawasaki's ER650 leading the way in sales. At the 2011 MGP Dave Moffitt won on a Suzuki, but at the TT it was a Kawasaki one-two-three thanks to Ryan Farquhar. Ryan had spotted the potential of the supertwins very early, and poured immense time and expertise into setting up bikes for himself and the other riders in his KMR racing team.

But Ryan and the rest of us had to wait, and wait some more, before seeing the new class line up on Glencrutchery Road. The race was scheduled for the morning of the final Friday with the Senior as usual in the afternoon. The day was damp, cold and miserable, and clerk of the course Gary Thompson wasted no time in abandoning the whole programme and rescheduling for the Saturday.

Twenty four hours later things were a little better, but conditions were far from ideal. The Lightweights eventually got going at 6.30pm, flagged off by MotoGP star Cal Crutchlow. Ryan was the strongest of favourites, and the only real drama concerned the various riders' pit strategy. In a three-lap race, some pitted after one lap, others after two. Ryan opted for the former strategy allowing James Hillier to take the lead, then when James pitted Ryan resumed his position and breezed in to win by 29 seconds from Hillier, with Rutter third. KMR bikes were first and third in the winners enclosure, and Hillier's ER650 was largely prepped by Ryan, so it was a brilliant evening for the Ulsterman.

It wasn't such a great day, alas, for those who'd been waiting a year to enjoy the daddy of them all, the Senior TT.

Where was the fat lady?

The day the Senior TT should have taken place was miserable and depressing. At the damp, grey paddock we were about as far as you can get from the usual bustling scene. Awnings were zipped up and bare patches had appeared where the sidecar crews had decamped. I dropped into the North One production HQ to see executive producer Neil Duncanson, and to pick up facts and figures about the North One operation which I planned to make use of next day. The next day was still overcast, still damp, but at least the rain had ceased and the track was drying. But would it dry quickly enough? Racing was postponed, and postponed again. Gary Thompson and some of the top riders toured the course and returned with long faces. The verdict: the Lightweight would go ahead, but the Senior ... no chance. Too many puddles, too many damp patches for the superbikes. For the first time in the history of the TT, the Senior machines would not go to the line.

What a strange feeling. No Senior race, and, therefore, no grand finale. Where was the fat lady, and what do you do if she does not sing? One thought that occurred to me was that it was quite surprising that we hadn't had bad weather on both the Friday and stand-by Saturday before, which would have caused a cancellation of the Senior some time ago. But, of course, it was only in the last seven or eight years or so that racing in the wet had been deemed unsafe for superbikes. In view of the amount of wet weather we get these days I began to wonder if the organisers should apply for permission to close the roads on the final Sunday as well, just in case. If not, a pattern of cancelled Seniors could well emerge in the next few years, and that would have a serious impact on the overall health of the TT.

It's so tricky, though. Any extension of the TT, even by 24 hours, would be unpopular with the big teams, especially Honda, whose boss Neil Tuxworth made little attempt to hide his frustration that the TT demanded so much time. Neil spent much of that Saturday in the media centre watching the action from Doha, where his Honda TT Legends were competing in the second round of the World Endurance Championship, a really bad clash of events with Neil and his riders John McGuinness, Cameron Donald and Gary Johnson all sitting around idly on the Isle of Man.

Hanging around in the commentary box, with little to do between updates on the weather and the track, was a surreal experience. We waited for decisions on the Senior while watching the paddock empty and the huge transporters navigate their way out onto Glencrutchery

Road, not their usual route, bottoming out as they tried to get up the ramp. The transporters had to get to the ferry port, but the usual exit from the paddock was obstructed by some of the essential raceday service vehicles which were still required. Kevin Evans, who did a great job running the paddock that year, had his work cut out.

There was time to reflect on the fact that this had been the least stressful TT of my time in the commentary box. No Guy Martin fireballs at Ballagarey, no Nicky Crowe disintegrations at Ballaugh, no red flags at all in the races and, praise be, no fatalities. But Guy was unusually low-profile in 2012, never looking like winning a race, and failing to get onto the rostrum for the first time since his debut season. I'd had a line up my sleeve for some years which I was going to use when he won a TT; now I began to doubt that it would ever be needed – which turned out to be true, although not exactly for the reasons I expected at the time! Cameron Donald also failed to win, but in contrast often looked likely to do so, and earned even more respect for the unfailingly cheerful, sportsmanlike way he accepted, three times, finishing in what's often called the most cruel position in sport, runner-up.

The possibility that this was my last day in the commentary box at the TT races didn't cross my mind that day. But it did when we reassembled on the island a few weeks later for the Manx Grand Prix.

It may well be that my complaint about the lack of information about riders, or my disinclination to bury debate about the MGP, or my criticism of the parade lap on my blog did not enhance my popularity in some quarters. Perhaps my comments were not viewed as constructive, even though my intention was only to express views which were helpful to the TT and the wider interests of the Isle of Man. Whatever, when I arrived for the Manx Grand Prix in August I was informed that someone in a position of authority had told a senior individual in Manx Radio that I was "a problem." And possibly a problem which might be harmful to Manx Radio's chances of renewing its contract, which was about to expire. I don't know who this person was, but I do know the comment was made, and, when it filtered through to me, it was unsettling. Throughout the MGP that year I felt I was standing on shifting sands. It's difficult to do a job which requires so many instant decisions and changes of tempo, and draws on such a wide range of emotions, if you don't feel you have the complete support of your management. I choose my words carefully here. I'm not saying that I didn't have that support. I might have done. But it didn't feel like it. As it happened, all the above demands were well and truly present at the 2012 MGP, not least when the supertwins race claimed the life of Trevor Ferguson, Ryan Farquhar's uncle who was riding Ryan's own bike. A week earlier I'd been chatting to Ryan at Tim and Jane Glover's wedding reception at Port Erin, and

Ryan had been looking forward to seeing Trevor race, and was also planning a winter racing campaign in Australia. The tragedy caused Ryan to rethink everything and step down from riding with immediate effect. A sad ending, but Ryan can be proud of an outstanding road racing career.

When the last race of the MGP was over, won sensationally by newcomer John Simpson, I closed Manx Radio's live coverage from the Mountain Course for another year. I had this gnawing feeling that it was the last time I would broadcast live from the commentary box above Glencrutchery Road. My final words were: "That's it. The end." And as I uttered them I knew I didn't just mean the race meeting.

2013 – A dream job for a sports broadcaster

Hitting the buffers

The 08.57 from Liverpool Lime Street was well on its way to Preston one morning in the second half of April 2013 when my mobile phone chirped. The read-out told me it was Manx Radio's main switchboard. I thought it would be Tim Glover. It was Anthony Pugh. I can't recall the conversation verbatim but the message will stay between my ears for ever. "Very sorry Charlie, but we will not be hiring you this year. We haven't got the money."

Anthony explained that there'd been tough talking between the radio station and the Department of Economic Development. One factor was that the DED required Manx Radio to put more resources into the new Classic TT at the end of August than it had previously done for the Manx GP. There were other financial pressures, and the upshot was that the budget didn't allow him to hire me, or Charlie Williams, or Mavis Brown or Heike Perry. He apologised for the relatively short notice, but up until the very last minute he'd been hoping that a deal would be done. Anthony sounded very upset, and I have no doubt that he made the phone call to me, as to the others, with a heavy heart. I don't think he wanted this outcome at all.

Fair enough. It was disappointing, but I had nothing to be bitter and twisted about. As I told Anthony at the time, I never thought when my stint as a TV reporter for the BBC came to an end that I'd have another nine years at the TT as chief commentator for the host broadcaster. I told him how grateful I was for that marvellous opportunity, and that is a sentiment I still feel today. Of course, I wish it could have been different, that Manx Radio could have found a pot of money to keep the old team together, but it wasn't cheap to pay for the travel and accommodation for Charlie and me, plus our wages. In any case, I've always recognised that any programme controller can make changes to the presentation team at any time; it happens frequently in our business for all kinds of reasons, and you just have to accept it.

Despite my pessimism at the end of the 2012 Manx Grand Prix, I'd been feeling quite upbeat in the early months of 2013. Towards the end of the November I rang Anthony and asked him straight out: "If Manx Radio does get the next TT contract, will I be part of your plans?" To which he answered yes, and told me to ensure I would be available. Then in February I received a text from Tim telling me to keep the TT dates free for work with Manx Radio. So I thought my worst fears were not going to be realised. But as the weeks went by with no confirmation, the doubts returned. A couple of days before Anthony's fateful phone call I rang him to ask what was going on. He couldn't give me a decision one way or the other. I said to Dorothy when I put the phone down: "I don't think we'll be there this year."

I understood Anthony's decision, accepted it completely, but it was still really hard to take. I didn't know if the various issues which had put one or two noses out of joint in 2012 had anything to do with it, but he told me the decision was made on financial grounds, and there was no arguing with that.

What made it all the tougher was that by mid-April I was already well under way with my preparation for the 2013 races. All my bookings were made, I'd been working on a new database, and I was planning to visit the North West-based teams SMT and Valmoto before crossing to the island. I'd recently bought a new lightweight printer to use with my laptop while at the races. I was also aware of an increasing amount of complimentary texts and tweets from listeners, including riders. People were starting to call me 'the Voice of the TT,' which was a supreme compliment. Duke Video used my commentary on its review of the 2012 TT, and Gaucho Productions did something similar in a documentary series on the Honda TT legends team. I felt I was more a part of the TT than ever. All of which made this the biggest disappointment of my broadcasting career, stretching over 35 years.

It was a setback when I was dropped as presenter of that sports programme on Radio 4 in the 1990s, but that was nothing like the hammer blow of losing the TT job. It was almost like a bereavement. For weeks I would wake up in the morning and the realisation would seep back into my mind, "I'm not the TT commentator any more." Sounds melodramatic now, but that is really how it was. My role with Radio TT was the glue that held together a lot of things that mattered a great deal: friendships, comradeship, my relationship with Manx Radio which stretched back to the Island Games in 2001, and included sending a bunch of broadcast students over to help run its service for the Commonwealth Youth Games in 2011. My involvement with the TT which went back to 1989/90, my affinity with the island itself, and my professional connection with motorbike racing. All ceased with that one phone call. Fortunately, a lot of friendships survive and I've since been back to the island for a family holiday, but it isn't the same.

"Now you know how Geoff Cannell felt," said Andy Wint when we had a coffee one day. Well, yes, and there's an obvious symmetry there. But I felt great empathy with Geoff at the time, and one big difference was that Geoff was still hugely involved as press officer after losing the commentator's role, whereas I was somewhat empty-handed.

Once the disappointment subsided it was replaced with a massive sense of frustration.

However, typical of the TT, the worst of times and the best of times walked hand in hand. The public response to my departure, and that of Charlie, Mavis and Heike, was simply overwhelming. More than once I found moisture in the eyes as a result of the incredibly kind and supportive comments that I was reading. Dozens of people left comments on my blog, and others left tweets and Facebook messages or emailed me directly. The *Isle of Man Examiner's* website received so many comments, nearly all supportive of me and the others, that the topic stayed on the home page of its website for days, and the TT's own online forum needed over 20 pages to accommodate the number of people who wanted to have their say. Manx Radio's Facebook page was brimful with complaints about our exits. There were more than a few calls for me to be reinstated, which was obviously nice to read but I knew it was never going to happen. I didn't encourage that idea because I knew all too well that my successor, Tim Glover, would find it challenging enough without that.

One TT fan posted a brilliant mock entry on the TT auction site, offering two "very rare pieces of TT memorabilia" for sale, namely me and Charlie Williams "with a couple of language translators included." We had a good chuckle at that.

The vast majority of messages were from people I've never met, and yet they all clearly felt some sort of affinity with me, Charlie, Mavis and Heike, and spoke volubly about how they felt something special was being taken away from them. I've never known anything like it. Any radio broadcaster would give their eye teeth for evidence of such a relationship with the listeners, so while I was gutted at the loss of the job, I was proud and grateful for the reaction.

I also received messages from the TT Riders Association and individual riders, the TT Supporters Club, plus its reps in France and Italy, well-known personalities within the TT organisation, fellow broadcasters and reporters, and road race fans from all over the world. I was offered accommodation and invited to spectate from people's front gardens. I thought there might be some sort of reaction, but absolutely nothing on the scale that developed. I can't thank everyone enough.

The dream job

TT 2013 was upon us before I had sorted out my emotions, and it was a tricky time. Tim was handed the commentator's role, with Chris Kinley taking over the chat show. I didn't think the radio station had given Tim anything like enough time to prepare. I gave him as much help and advice as I felt able to. I couldn't imagine not being on the island, and Dorothy and I went over for the pre-TT at Billown and the start of Practice Week. We touched base with a lot of people, said a lot of thank-yous, and had a lovely dinner with Mavis, her husband, Clive, and Heike. We spent some time with my pal, Alan Knight, and his partner, Jackie, who were incredibly supportive throughout the whole situation. Gillian Bowers and her husband, Ned, former MGP winner and now a travelling marshal, were very generous and hospitable. We had a good few days, but couldn't stay for the whole event. I'd been a full-time senior lecturer at the University of Central Lancashire since 2006, but at the end of May every year I'd put the TT first. Now it was only right to reverse that and attend to university commitments. So, like the rest of the worldwide audience, I followed TT 2013 by listening online and following the live timing service.

And it was all going well until the Monday afternoon of Race Week when I was listening in my university office. I became aware of my colleague, Amy Binns, who shares the office, saying "Charlie, why are you growling at your computer?" I didn't realise I was making any sound. I was listening to the commentary on the Superstock TT. I could see that some of the information coming across the radio didn't match the data on the live timing, and I was getting anxious. It was a bit difficult explaining to Amy that something strange was going on between the Hairpin and the Bungalow!

That was the day Michael Dunlop won two TTs in a day, and it was the only time I felt really low during my first TT as an off-island listener. It hurt to be missing out on describing Michael's superlative performances that day. It was like being the only one not invited to a party. I got home to Liverpool and moaned to Dorothy, who's seen all the ups and downs over the years.

"Most people will think it was just another job," she said.

It was never that.

Being TT commentator from 2004 to 2012 was an exciting, challenging, emotional, demanding privilege. This is one of the oldest motorsport events in the world. It is unique. Its reliance on the power of radio to tell everyone what is happening makes it a dream job for a sports broadcaster. I am lucky to have become the second longest-serving lead commentator in the history of Manx Radio, and the only non-Manxman to be entrusted with the task. I described 193 races in my time, encompassing the first 130mph lap, the first 131mph lap, the first sub-20-minute sidecar lap, the still-to-be-threatened outright sidecar lap record, the Centenary TT, the Mountain Course Centenary, the first podium by a woman at the MGP, the first victory by a woman at the MGP, the second-closest finish of a TT race, the closest-ever finish over the Mountain Course, the first TT for electric bikes, the first 100mph electric lap, the only five-out-of-five winner, the unique Billown two-stroke TTs and many more historic moments. Away from the commentary box I was proud to be asked to lead the funeral of Paul Dobbs, to contribute to *TT3D: Closer to the Edge*, to introduce the film and its stars and producer at the première in Douglas, and to attend two receptions at Government House. And I met the most courageous sportsmen and women in the world.

And finally, my top-twenty Mountain Course moments

There were countless memorable moments in the Radio TT commentary box – most of them relating to the action taking place outside the windows, but some of them to do with what was happening in our own little unit. These are my top 20. They originally appeared in more detail on my blog, and cover both the TT and MGP.

1: The Junior Manx Grand Prix race in 2006. The first two riders to leave the line side by side are Yorkshire's Craig Atkinson and Ireland's Derek Brien. They get the tap on the shoulder at the same time, they depart at the same time. After three laps, with one circuit of the mountain to go, there are only seven-tenths of a second between them, Atkinson leading. This can never happen again – riders no longer start in pairs at either the MGP or TT. Past Ramsey and over Snaefell it is still nip and tuck, neither man able to make a decisive break. This is going to be closer than close. I lock my gaze onto the tarmac of Glencrutchery Road and the Honda of Atkinson and the Kawasaki of Brien scream into view, still cheek by jowl as if strapped by gaffer tape. This is no time to be waiting for the computer to process the information, I call it as I see it: Atkinson. Even though I'm watching at an angle and not dead in line, I'm sure Craig has won it. Then the computer has its say: Atkinson, by one hundredth of a second. One hundredth of a second! Phew! And what drama! The adrenalin is still fizzing days later and that's only the commentator! Without doubt the most exciting moment I've known in live broadcasting, anywhere. And that's why Craig Atkinson's duel with the equally brilliant Derek Brien at the MGP 2006 is my number one Mountain Memory.

2: John McGuinness and his lap record in the Superbike TT 2004, my very first Radio TT commentary. John's average speed of 127.68mph slashes 3.2 seconds off the previous best set by David Jefferies two years earlier.

3: These are my most memorable moments, not necessarily the happiest, and this is one of the toughest situations I had to deal with – the crash involving six-time winner Nicky Crowe and twice-winner Mark Cox in the second Sidecar TT in 2009. Horrendous suspense followed by relief and gratitude that they'd survived.

4: Fourth place goes to one of the moments that make the job so exciting – when the time trial nature of the races really comes into its own, and it's too close to call as the riders head down from Cronk ny Mona on the last lap. It's 2012, and the first of the 600cc Supersport races won by Bruce Anstey from Cameron Donald by just 0.77 seconds.

5: Another Magnificent McGuinness moment. The first 130mph lap, recorded at the Centenary TT in 2007.

6: Ian Hutchinson emerges triumphant in the four-lap restarted Senior TT 2010, leading from flag to flag with two 131mph laps in the first two, to complete his historic five out of five.

7: A different kind of history but just as remarkable. The Ultra-Lightweight MGP in 2009. It's the midway point in the race and riders are coming in for the routine pit stop. Carolynn Sells' bright orange Yamaha FZR400 rockets into view – but does not slow down. She scorches past the pit wall, head down. What's happening? A desperate blunder or a brilliant strategy? All is revealed soon enough. Brilliant strategy. The Paul Morrissey/Martin Bullock team has calculated their fuel consumption to the drop, and without a pit stop Carolynn wins the race and I'm saluting the first woman ever (and still) to win a solo race around the Mountain Course. Afterwards we examine the stats again and work out that she would still have won even with a pit stop.

8: Another entry for John McGuinness as he slows into pit lane at the end of lap two of the 2009 Senior TT, having set a new outright lap record of 131.578mph.

9: Two for the price of one. Every now and then a rider runs out of gas or hits some other problem right at the end of a race and has to push the machine several hundred yards to the finish. When there's a podium place at stake it is incredibly dramatic, and this is what happens in the Manx GP Lightweight Classic 2011 as Maria Costello is spotted pushing the 250cc Bob Jackson Suzuki T20. She makes it to the line to clinch third place, and become the first woman to achieve two podium places on the Mountain Course. Even more dramatic as we fast-forward to 2012 and Chris Palmer has a real task on his hands, pushing the 500cc Ripley Land Matchless G50. He's still in the hunt for a place on the rostrum, but it's a warm day and a heavy load. The crowd cheer him on and he just reaches the finish before collapsing on the tarmac. No lasting damage, and he has third place as his reward.

10: The second Supersport TT in 2009. A 21-year-old with a famous name. Michael Dunlop is competing in only his third TT, and has never been on the podium, but on this day he puts in a final lap of 125.077mph to win the race on his Streetsweep/Marlow Construction Yamaha R6. The start of something big.

11: Carl Fogarty leads off a parade lap to mark 50 years of Ducati. Never one to shirk the spotlight when he's on a motorbike, Foggy instantly pulls the most extravagant of wheelies and sashays down Glencrutchery Road. Star quality.

12: Chris Kinley's famous "chain's off the sprocket" aria as Richard Britton sets off after his second pit stop in the Senior TT in 2005.

13: Dave Molyneux and Dan Sayle's slow-motion sidecar victory in 2005.

14: Nicky Crowe and Dan Sayle setting a new sidecar lap record of 116.667mph in 2007.

15: Not a moment in the actual commentary box but in a virtual commentary box in the Goldcrest studios in London, dubbing commentary onto the soundtrack of the movie *TT3D: Closer to the Edge*.

16: Norman Quayle's unintended jape in 2011 when he handed me a note reading "a new lap record," except it actually read "not a new lap record," but he managed to cover the word "not" with his thumb.

17: Cueing-in Murray Walker for his commentary on the parade lap at the Mountain Course centenary, 2011.

18: The second Sidecar TT in 2011 and Robin and Annette Daykin claim finishers' medals against more odds than even Ladbrokes could dream up.

19: That crazy behind-the-scenes incident when Mavis Brown tripped over a cable and fell headlong while I was live on air.

20: The start of the Superbike TT 2008, and the panic-stricken moment when Guy Martin was late for the start having been delayed in the toilet.

Check out these other motorcycle books from Veloce:

Essential Buyer's Guides:

www.veloce.co.uk

Restoration manuals:

Index

ACU 59, 80
Agostini, Giacomo 40, 56, 70, 98
Alflatt, Brian 54
Allison, Bob 22, 70, 124
Amor, Keith 58, 69, 98, 111, 112, 123, 126, 128, 131
Andrews, Simon 131
Anstey, Bruce 16, 39, 40, 47, 54, 61, 68-70, 72, 98, 99, 110, 113, 123, 125-127, 129, 138-140, 152
Archibald, Adrian 16, 27, 39, 56, 68-70, 72, 123
Armstrong, Ian 58
Atkinson, Craig 43, 107, 126, 139, 151
Aylott, Mike 64, 129, 138

Baker, Tony 21, 53
Baker-Milligan, Fiona 20, 21, 53
Ball, Mike 14
Barber, Rob 73, 101, 103, 141
Barclay, Adam 107
Barker, Stuart 61
Barks, Samantha 73
Barron, Debbie 142
Barth, Markus 26
Beattie, Nigel 29
Beck, Simon 30
Bell, David and Susan 36
Bell, Ian 41, 51
Bennett, Garry 25
Bentley, Ashley 18
Biggs, Phil 34, 108
Biggs, Vince 108

Binns, Amy 149
Birchall, Ben and Tom 138, 141
Bird, Paul 48
Birdsall, Barry and John 38
Bitter, Sandor 123
Bolliger, Hans-Peter 58
Bolster, April 29
Bond, Stuart 41
Bonetti, Stefano 33
Bowers, Gillian and Ned 149
Brien, Derek 43, 126, 127, 139, 151
Britton, Richard 24, 27, 28, 153
Brouwer, Ferry 131
Brown, Mavis 48, 114, 135, 146, 148, 149, 153
Brown, Tony 52
Bryan, Gary 99
Buckley, Mark 138
Bullock, Martin 32, 47, 48, 107, 108
Burns, Darren 60
Burrows, John 104, 130

Cannell, Geoff 8, 10-14, 48, 74, 135, 148
Carpenter, Neil 41
Carswell, Gary 16, 58, 107
Cavendish, Mark 71, 104
Challenger, Ben 138
Charnock, Mick 38
Chauhan, Dipash 53, 141
Christian, Dave 107, 128, 139

Christian, Louis 64
Christian, Steve 122, 123
Clague, Trisha 22
Clark, Dan 34, 53, 63, 64
Clark, Dave 35
Clark, Les and Stella 34
Clarke, Fred 12
Closer to the Edge 121, 122, 150, 153
Clucas, Tommy 32
Collier, Charles 47, 49, 57
Conti, Angelo 33
Cooper, Marc 125
Corkish, Geoff 109
Costello, Maria 25, 78, 152
Coughlan, David 25
Coward, Jamie 108
Coward, Paul 108
Cox, Mark 64-66, 99-101, 152
Craig, Wilson 123, 124
Crellin, John 104
Crellin, Mike 111
Crellin, Simon 12, 46, 97, 114
Cretney, David 10
Cross, Lawrence 38
Crossan, Adrian 71
Crowe, Nick 18, 19, 41, 51, 52, 64-66, 99-101, 116, 144, 152, 153
Crutchlow, Cal 142
Cubbon (also Crossley), Eunice 7, 16, 18, 27, 50, 58, 97, 103, 134, 135
Cubbon, Mark 103
Cummins, Carol 119
Cummins, Conor 58, 62, 67,

68, 98, 99, 104, 110, 113, 119, 122, 123, 125
Currie, Bill 64
Czysz, Michael 116

Dainese, Lino 67
Daykin, Robin and Annette 129, 130, 153
De Aragues, Richard 122, 123
Dix, Matt 117
Dobbs, Bridget 118, 119, 123
Dobbs, Paul 117-119, 150
Doherty, Ken 34
Donald, Cameron 38, 40, 61, 68, 69, 72, 73, 75, 110, 113, 123, 124-126, 128, 138-140, 144, 152
Dongworth, Phil 100
Doyle, Craig 109
Duke, Geoff 61
Dukes, Nicky 117
Duncan, Uel 38
Duncanson, Neil 143
Dunlop, Joey 38
Dunlop, Michael 60, 71, 73, 98, 99, 110-112, 123, 126, 127, 138-140, 149, 153
Dunlop, Robert 25, 60
Dunlop, William 60, 119, 124, 140

Elkins, Christian 60
Elmer, Tony 129
Energy FM 13-15, 106
Evans, Kevin 71, 144

Farmer, Mark 30
Farrelly, Peter 65
Farquhar, Ryan 16, 22, 27, 33, 40, 54, 62, 73, 98, 111, 113, 123, 138-140, 142, 144, 145
Farrance, Patrick 64, 116, 138, 142
Fazackerley, Graham 137
Fenwick, Ted 108
Ferguson, George 12, 13
Ferguson, Trevor 144, 145
Fern, Andy 19, 66
Finnegan, Martin 24, 25, 28, 54, 59, 70, 71
Fisher, Rob 52
Fogarty, Carl 47, 57, 73, 153
Founds, Peter 53
Fowler, Rem 47, 49, 102
Fraser, Jem 131

Gasse, Harald 115
Gawne, Phil 10
Gilmore, Victor 107
Gittere, CR 77, 133
Glover, Tim 7, 44, 45, 62, 63, 75, 77, 100, 103-105, 109, 144, 147-149
Godart, Etienne 48
Gorst, Adrian 125
Granié, Marc 26
Grant, Mick 49
Greene, Seamus 36
Greenlight TV 66
Griffiths, Jason 39, 40

Hailwood, David 72
Hailwood, Mike 70-72, 100
Hallam, Craig 36
Hanks, Roy 41, 53
Hanks, Tom 34
Hanson, Neil 14, 47, 59
Harah, Les 29
Hardy, Graham 131
Harrison, Conrad 129, 138
Harvey, Mick 20, 21
Harvey, Phil 20,21
Hawes, Dick 20, 53
Heath, Chas 38
Heath, Chris 35, 103
Heron, Tony 70
Hideyuki, Yoshida 54
Hillier, James 73, 104, 142
HM Plant Honda 37, 50, 61
Holden, John 41, 51, 52, 64-66, 75, 76, 99, 100, 129, 130, 138
Honda TT Legends 123, 125, 143
Hope, Darren 18, 19, 41
Horspole, Gary 53
Hunt, Paul 27
Hurst, Roger 59
Hussain, Azhar 102, 115
Hussey, Trevor 136, 137
Hutchinson, Ian 29, 37, 39, 40, 49, 50, 54, 56, 61, 62, 68, 70, 73, 98, 99, 108-113, 122-125, 132, 152

Isle of Man Examiner 10, 41, 148

Jackson, Alan 'Bud' 14
Jacob, Dean 45
Jamieson, Geraldine 74
Jefferies, David 15-16, 30, 131, 152

Jefferies, Nick 131
Jefferies, Pauline 54
Johnson, Gary 58, 69, 73, 76, 125, 126, 128, 139, 143

Karlsson, Joakim 29, 31
Kenzig, Greg 45
Kermode, Adrian 110
Kermode, Paul 66
Kiff, Eddie 20
Kinley, Chris 7, 14, 22, 27, 28, 44, 48, 49, 65, 66, 73, 74, 77, 105, 109, 129, 134, 149, 153
Klaffenbock, Klaus 51, 52, 66, 99, 116, 117, 126, 129, 138
Kneale, Peter 8, 11-12, 30, 61, 74, 135
Kneen, Dan 98, 104
Knight, Alan 7, 149
Knight, Dan 117
Knight, David 137
Knight, Gary 117
Knights, Richie 76
Kniveton, Colin 135
Kuehn, Stefan 58
Kumano, Masato 54

Laidlow, Ruth 53
Lambert, Dorothy 7, 37, 44, 45, 70, 77, 108, 117, 147, 149
Lambert, Greg 34
Last-Sutton, Simon 66
Le Moal, Serge 30
Leblond, Francois and Sylvie 56
Lines, Michael 63, 64
Linsdell, Olie 73
Linsdell, Steve 25, 57, 73
Linton, Dick 108
Lockey, Wayne 130
Lofthouse, Mick 30
Loicht, Martin 115, 117
Long, Rick 34, 52
Lougher, Ian 22, 24, 27, 28, 38, 55, 74, 105, 111
Lynch, Cedric 102

Macfadyen, Ian, Lt Gov 23, 24
Mackman, Ian 73, 104, 132
Maeda, Jun 28, 29, 36
Manx Motorcycle Club 31, 42, 57, 59, 135, 137
Manx Grand Prix 7, 25, 27-29, 32, 43, 78, 111, 114, 135-

137, 142, 144, 145, 150, 152
Manx Radio 7, 10-14, 21, 48, 75, 106, 112, 124, 134, 135, 144, 146-148, 150
Marsom, John 77
Marshall, Darren 129
Martin, Guy 27, 28, 49-51, 54, 55, 57, 61, 63, 67-70, 72, 79, 80, 98, 104, 110-112, 123, 125, 126, 128, 129, 144, 153
Mawdsley, Kevin 33
Mawdsley, Marilyn 63
Mawdsley, Maurice 8, 16, 21, 37, 50, 62, 63, 68, 72, 75, 99, 104, 135
Mayers, Nigel 53
McAdoo Racing 38, 125
McBride, James 58, 71
McCallen, Philip 79
McCrea, Kenny 33
McGladdery, Andy 16, 19, 29
McGuinness, John 15, 24, 27, 28, 35, 37, 39, 40, 44, 46, 47, 49-51, 54, (130mph lap) 56, 57, 60, 61, 67-72, 98, 99, 104, 110, 112, 113, 123-126, 128, 129, 132, 138, 141, 143, 151, 152
Mercer, Steve 103
Migout, Fabienne 78
Miguet, Fabrice 56
Miller, Jason 65
Miller, Mark 102, 141
Mister, Lloyd 142
Moffitt, Dave 142
Molyneux, Dave 16-18, 36, 41, 51, 52, 64-66, 99, 100, 116, 126, 138, 141, 142, 153
Molyneux, Gaynor 52
Moore, Jimmy 58
Moore, Roy 19, 21, 48, 52, 65, 74, 100, 104, 107, 122, 124, 128
Moorley, Glenn 113
Montano, Thomas 102
Moralee, William 117
Motorcycle News 42, 43, 135
Moyle, Michael 59
Muir, Shaun 123

Neary, Simon 41, 53, 66, 100
Neill, Hector 64
Nelson, Eddie 78, 79, 128, 129
Nilsson, Mats 73, 77, 107, 115

Norbury, Steve 18-19, 41, 52, 53, 66
NW 200 60, 77, 124

Orritt, Paul 31
Owen, Gareth 76
Owen, Paul 24, 45, 76, 77

Padgett, Clive 125
Padgett's Racing Team 61, 109
Palmer, Chris 16, 29, 74, 111, 152
Parrett, Mark 55, 73, 107, 128
Patel, Hassan 46
Patoni, Roberto 57
Patricot, Hubert 99
Pattinson, Ian 48, 58, 73
Perry, Heike 16, 48, 117, 135, 146, 148, 149
Petty, Chris 103
Phillips, Paul 24, 76
Pike, Chris 125
Plater, Steve 51, 58, 62, 69, 72, 98-100, 104, 107
Porter, Raymond 27
Price, Robert 25, 26
Pugh, Anthony 11, 48, 58, 77, 146, 147

Quayle, Milky 24, 137
Quayle, Norman 15, 51, 63, 103, 126, 135, 153

Ramsbotham, Marc 44
Read, Phil 70
Redmond, Derek 138
Reeves, Tim 65, 100, 105, 123, 141
Rennie, Carl 73, 104
Reynolds, John 70
Reynolds, Mike 70
Richardson, Roy 108, 119
Robinson, Jamie 73
Roper, Dave 131
Rossi, Valentino 79, 80, 98
Rostron, Brian and Ann 20
Rutter, Michael 56, 130, 141, 142

Sawyer, Geoff 32
Sayle, Dan 16-18, 36, 41, 51, 52, 65, 66, 99, 105, 116, 117, 126, 129, 141, 153
Schoenfelder, Thomas and Simone 58
Schofield, Allan 52, 53

Scott, Gus 29
Sells, Carolynn 78, 107, 152
Silvester, Robbie 24, 33, 78
Simpson, John 145
Smallwood, Heather 136
Snelling, Bill 61
Southwick, Sam 122
Spence, George 72
Spenner, Frank 46
Stewart, Dan 73
Surtees, John 47, 57
Swallow, Bill 107

TAS Suzuki 16, 39, 54, 64, 69, 110
Tapken, Dick 53
Taveri, Luigi 131
Taylor, Jock 66
Taylor, Merita 139
Taylor, Steve 21
Thompson, Gary 142, 143
Tinmouth, Jenny 78, 98
Truelove, Josie 71
Turner, Juan 13, 14
Tuxworth, Neil 143

Ubbiali, Carlo 73

Van Gils, Patrick 26
Vanderhaar, James 78
Vloemans, Bert 70

Wain, Phil 7, 130
Walker, Dan 135
Walker, Murray 47, 54, 130, 131, 153
Wallis, Dave 64
Warner, Alan 70
Watanabe, Masahito 54
Weynand, Michael 33, 58
Whitham, James 72
Williams, Charlie 14, 48, 107, 108, 131, 136, 146, 148
Williams, Chris 22
Williams, Peter 102
Wilson, Scott 107
Winkle, Andy 64, 65, 74, 75, 99, 129
Wint, Andy 7, 11, 106, 148
Wolfenden, Eric and Stella 106, 119
Wood, Adam, Lt Gov 122
Woods, Stanley 40
Wouters, Bert 70
Wright, Doug 53
Wright, Eddy 53